SAMUEL J WOFF

MODERN LITIGATION

How, How Much and Why?

GRIGSONPUBLISHING.COM

Published by

Grigson Publishing

ISBN: 978-0-6456593-8-2

Cover design, illustration and interior formatting:
Mark Thomas / Coverness.com

For my family, Linda and Wayne, Megan, Charlotte, Alex,
and for Jenny, my love.

CONTENTS

FOREWORD i

INTRODUCTION III

PART 1: HOW 1

CHAPTER 1 - ADVICE OR ADVOCACY 3

CHAPTER 2 – WHAT HAPPENED? 15

CHAPTER 3 - TYPES OF DISPUTES 26

CHAPTER 4 - VALUING, IMPROVING AND CONVEYANCING 35

CHAPTER 5 - CREATIVITY 48

CHAPTER 6 - SETTLING 66

PART 2: HOW MUCH 75

CHAPTER 7 - WHY SELL? 77

CHAPTER 8 - REJECTION 84

CHAPTER 9 - STATISTICS TELL THE STORY 92

CHAPTER 10 - IN DEFENCE OF THE BILLABLE HOUR 103

CHAPTER 11 - A FIXED FEE? 115

CHAPTER 12 – NO WIN, NO FEE? 126

CHAPTER 13 - REDUCING LEGAL COSTS 131

PART 3: WHY 141

CHAPTER 14 - TIME, COST AND QUALITY 143

CHAPTER 15 - WHO'S ON YOUR TEAM? 159

CHAPTER 16 - THE STRENGTH OF THE FIRM 167

CHAPTER 17 - ENFORCEMENT 181

CHAPTER 18 - THE IMPORTANCE OF INCENTIVES 193

CONCLUSION 219

ACKNOWLEDGEMENTS 221

THE MISSING INGREDIENT 225

FOREWORD

I became a teacher by accident. After finishing my law degree, I had to complete two years of National Service. A few months later, one of the education officers approached me and asked if I would like to do a spot of teaching. I very cautiously responded, "Teaching what to whom?" He told me someone needed to fill in for an English teacher who had been working with apprentices, but he had been posted elsewhere.

I accepted and, as it turned out, I couldn't have enjoyed it more. At the end of my stint of "Nasho", I completed a teaching qualification and landed a job almost immediately. That was the beginning of over forty years in a career that I could not have enjoyed more for the opportunity it gave me to work alongside those students with obvious emerging talent.

In 1980, I took up a post at Caulfield Grammar School, teaching English and Legal Studies. It was there in 2003 that I met Samuel Woff, one of those unnerving students who managed to know the answer to a question before the teacher finished asking it. Samuel took to Legal Studies with extraordinary enthusiasm, as he did with all the school offered him, and achieved outstanding results.

I always knew that Samuel would write a book, and I am utterly delighted that Modern Litigation serves as a splendid guidebook on the mindset necessary to be a successful litigation lawyer. It is written precisely and with great clarity.

In the 1960s, I remember reading The Art of the Advocate by Richard Du

Cann, QC. It was an inspirational book for its time, and I have no doubt that Modern Litigation by Samuel J. Woff will be equally as inspirational for law students and practitioners in the 2020s and beyond.

David S. Thomson, OAM, FACE
Fellow, The Sir Zelman Cowen Centre
Victoria University

INTRODUCTION

A successful career as a litigator requires three things, each of which relates to a horizon of focus:

- Near term, we have to get the best result on the *current* case (the ***How***).
- Medium-term, we need to have an eye towards wining the mandate for the next case, as well as making enough money to pay the bills (the ***How Much***).
- Finally, long term, we have an obligation, as guardians of the legal profession (being temporary caretakers for but a while before passing the baton on), to contribute back to the health and vitality of the profession as a whole (the ***Why***).

The chapters of this book follow the same delineation. In Part One (How), we look at today's problems: how to *win* this case. Once our current objectives are under control, we tilt our heads slightly upwards to look further along the path to tomorrow's problems. Winning the right to handle the next case and issues of compensation. These 'tomorrow' focused challenges comprise Part Two (How Much) of this book.

Finally, there is Part Three (Why), and this division of the book tackles the wider issues surrounding the profession as a whole. We take in the entire horizon here. While this may feel broad and remote from our day-to-day, don't be misled into thinking this big-picture stuff is someone else's problem – the profession's health is the going concern of every current member. Because it grapples with large and important subjects, this last Part of the book is by necessity the most ambitious: it looks at how the profession might be uplifted, improved, and integrated into the successful progress of civilisation. I trust this is both interesting and inspiring food for thought.

A note before starting

Before commencing, an opening remark.

To the extent that objective "best practice" is identifiable in the indefinitely nuanced practice of law, the earlier chapters of this book attempt to distil and present it. These concepts are readily identifiable (and testable) against our own experience, and indeed, it is from my experience that the content of these chapters is gleaned. I, therefore, present these earlier chapters to the extent I am (or indeed anyone is) positioned as the authoritative "best way of doing things".

As we journey through the book, however, and especially in the later chapters, as we consider a wider lens of focus, we depart from the realm of objective fact and into the arena of subjective opinion. The issue to do with (to a lesser extent) money and marketing and (to a much greater extent) the vector of the profession as a whole do not readily lend themselves to a single discernible correct answer. In this way, I present the later chapters as a point of view only, one among potentially many. To borrow the distinction to be discussed in Chapter 1, these chapters advocate for a position. They do not provide objective advice.

This, of course, does not invalidate the contents of those chapters – by necessity, many books (especially in the political sciences) are a thesis of informed opinions rather than objective facts. But it does benefit the reader, I think, to be clear-eyed about this distinction, lest they be beguiled into elevating the words to gospel status. The later chapters present *arguments*, not necessarily universal truths.

This should be a concept of comfort for most lawyers, as most litigation is a battle to find the best argument rather than (necessarily) the closest version of objective truth. But, in the context of reading a book as opposed to battling in court, it does warrant a slight change of approach. As lawyers, when confronted with an *argument*, our almost intuitive approach is to come up with numerous reasons it doesn't work, cross our arms and stubbornly reject it. This is fine and often entirely appropriate in this courtroom and what we are paid to do.

However, outright unthinking rejection does leave our mindset rather impervious to new ideas. I, therefore, suggest a subtle re-orientation in approach. When presented with the *arguments* in this book, rather than adopt the truculent attitude of opposing counsel, adopt the judicious and discerning attitude of the judge. *Consider* and *weigh* the argument, then form a view rather than simply defaulting to our base instinct to reject it summarily.

PART 1
HOW

CHAPTER 1 - ADVICE OR ADVOCACY

"Start With Why"

- Simon Sinek (2009)

Why have we been hired? There are only two possible answers: advice or advocacy.

Advocacy

Advocacy is the quintessential legal task. When a lawyer is mentioned, it is an advocate who is mentally conjured, and fictional characters such as Atticus Finch and Lt. Daniel Caffey pounding court tables are evoked. Advocacy means lawyers making arguments, fighting cases and chasing justice. In court and out.

Undoubtedly, it's a glamorous caricature. It fuels fictional adaptations and law school enrolments, and, such is its attractiveness, the image is often adopted as the spokesperson for the profession as a whole. The fearless litigator. A knight for justice. An example of a *good* lawyer.

A knight is a good analogy because the lawyer is in battle when advocating.

Litigation is (bloodless) warfare.[1] Advocates *fight* for their clients. Your opponents are the *enemy*. There are litigation *strategies* and courtroom *tactics*. We hit witnesses and arguments with *attacks*, parry with *defences*, and ultimately prevail *victorious* or leave *defeated*. No doubt, it's war. The qualities of a good advocate should, therefore mirror those of a good warrior: skill, courage and daring—tenacity, valour and grit.

But the indispensable trait? Passion. Advocates don't have to act it (passion is *not* commensurate with hysterics, shouting and tantrums), but they must certainly *feel* it. War is no time for apathy. To be effective, an excellent litigator must carry their papers into court, as well as a passionate soul, a fire in their eye and a hot heart beating in their chest.

After all, it's a battle. You must be fired up. Hence the *haka*. The best advocacy is always imbued with an undercurrent of emotional force because if you don't passionately believe in your argument, why would anyone else?

Advisor

Then there's the quieter, stiller, and less glamourous part of being a lawyer: rendering advice, listening, considering and explaining, informing and making recommendations. Guiding clients in the right direction. *Here are your legal rights. Here are the costs and benefits of going to court. And here's what I recommend.*

While advocacy is the treatment, advice is the diagnosis and prescription, the preliminary step. It provides answers to the questions: Where do I stand? And what should I do?

Advice requires performing investigations, outlining options and making a recommendation. The advice *might* be to go to court, but not always. The court is just one treatment option. The advice might also be to go home! Doing nothing is better.

Advisors must listen carefully, have the knowledge and (ideally) some bedside manners. However, most crucially, advisors need a detached mindset.

1 With thanks to the inimitable Irving Younger for this observation.

Logic, reason and facts must drive recommendations – never emotion. For this reason, they discourage doctors from advising family members. Emotion sabotages the clear thinking required.

So, while advocacy requires passion and fire, advice requires the opposite. Rationality, balance, and an unencumbered mind. In short, a cool head.

Other differences

The differences continue.

Advisors must acknowledge the strengths and weaknesses of a client's case to advise on whether the court is worthwhile. They must be balanced. On the other hand, advocates are persuaders, and persuasion demands conveying the impression that issues are cut and dry, black and white, open and shut in favour of their client. So, while advisors see nuance, advocates prefer absolutes. To be convincing, you must be sure.

(This is a good test: if you can see and acknowledge both sides of the argument, you are probably advising. Suppose you have condemned and damned any view contradicting your own as incompatible with the objective truth of the universe. In that case, you have probably drifted into advocacy).

To be convincing, you must be sure.

The purpose of facts is different. Facts are a tool of diagnosis for the advisor but a tool of *argument* for the advocate. Good advice requires all the facts, unvarnished, whereas good advocacy is content with selected facts and coloured interpretations.

Good advice *predicts* the outcome of a court case. Good advocacy *influences* it.

Advisors take the back seat – the client must ultimately decide what to do (it's just "advice", after all). But advocates drive. During the case's lifetime, advocates have complete discretion to run the case as they consider appropriate.

Advisors must be intellectually correct, while advocates seek victory. Importantly, these things are not necessarily co-extensive.

Advisors must always consider the benefits and costs of litigating. At the same time, advocates (in the battle) are better unencumbered by such considerations. Military effectiveness is likely to be hampered if soldiers must constantly double-guess whether they (or their taxpayers) can really afford to fire a particular missile.

Advice is a one-on-one human interaction and requires commensurate interpersonal skills. The advocate, on the other hand, is theatrical. They are on the stage. A larger-than-life presence is necessary, while a pleasant, nice bedside manner can be somewhat superfluous.

If the advisor does their job correctly, they may have to deliver some blunt truth early ("you have no case"). Conversely, even in the face of massive challenges, the advocate can bracingly reassure the client that 'we will do our best' and can defer the delivery of bad news to a later point, and even then, only if the case is lost.

Advising is an analytical task of synthesising facts with the law to come to a logical conclusion on likely court outcomes. At the other end of the spectrum, advocates generate arguments. While this is founded on facts and law, it is ultimately an exercise in *creativity*, not simple logic.

Advisors benefit from knowing the client well. An intimate understanding of the patient's circumstances ensures that recommendations are tailored. Conversely, advocates can remain impersonal and aloof. The treatment and the arguments in court remain the same regardless.

The need for both

Despite the differences, as advice is the diagnosis and advocacy is the treatment, clients clearly need both. Advice without treatment cannot cure you, while treatment without advice can make you worse.

Advice without treatment cannot cure you, while treatment without advice can make you worse.

However, even though the client needs both, it is hard for one lawyer to *be* both.

The *skills* are different, but that's not fatal. Skills are learnable. More insurmountable is that the necessary *mindsets* are at divergent ends of the spectrum.

Fierce advocacy backed by emotion, against cool advice better impervious to the same. Passion, fight and grit versus being cool, calculating and intellectual. Influencing the outcome or predicting it. Being persuasive or being correct. Front seat or back.

Doing both is difficult. How can you successfully switch from the hot heart to the cool head and back without allowing any residual temperature from one leak across to the other?

The reality is to be *both* an excellent advocate and an excellent advisor, the lawyer must prevent what makes them successful in one arena from infecting the other. The roles must be kept quarantined. Heat in advice is fatal to accuracy, while hesitancy in advocacy destroys an advocate's ability to be persuasive.

A challenge? Indeed! It is a tension requiring some cognitive disassociation to navigate. It's not easy containing the passion that makes you a successful litigator when advising, and equally hard to ignite passion on demand to advocate if you are more familiar with calculating advice.

The result is that many lawyers pick (often subconsciously). Batting and bowling require different skills, so cricketers specialise. And so it is here. Either you advocate or advise. The delicate switching process and different mental positioning required make it difficult to be good at both.

Choosing advocacy

Faced with the choice, many lawyers prefer advocacy. Why?

- More money
- More glory
- Less hard work

Let's examine each.

Money

Advocates generally make more money.

It's easier to get hired. Clients who come to a lawyer with a grievance often want their lawyer to reflect their belligerent mindset. They want an ally, a champion and a partisan advocate. They want to hear their lawyer say: "*Don't worry, we'll smash them for you*". Yeah! In their aggrieved state of mind, clients often *want* to take someone down. They want "*justice*". They want to prepare for battle.

They often don't want to hear such pernickety statements as, "*let's think through the various options and the pros and cons*", even if (and sometimes especially if) completely accurate.

Hence, clients often gravitate towards advocates, fearless and fearsome warriors ready to indulge their psychological preference to fight instead of a more circumspect advisor.

Alternatively, the stakes are so high in some cases that the litigants *have* to go to court. Suppose you are fighting over a billion dollars. In that case, you don't need an advisor to assess the costs and benefits of going to court. You are going. And if you are going, you need an advocate.

Moreover, once hired, advocacy work is lucrative. Lawyers sell time, and litigation takes plenty. While the advice is in and out, litigation can last years.

That lawyers are often paid for each hour regardless of the result of the case reinforces, rather than regulates, this tendency.

Glory

Easier to get hired and more profitable. That's an attractive economic proposition. Compounding the fiscal incentives is the fact that being an advocate appeals to many lawyers' professional predilections.

It's very glamorous to be an advocate. Fame and glory go to the advocate that wins the case. "*The lawyers who get the headlines are the ones that 'ride in and slay the dragon*'", says Bruce MacEwen, the founder of Adam Smith Esq, the consulting firm.[2] Reputations go to fearsome litigators. Movie adaptations go to those victorious in the courtroom. Client gratitude extends to winners.

It's much harder to achieve fame by dishing out meticulous but uninspiring advice in the back office. Few litigators dream of being the world's best advice renderer – most want to be famous for winning.

Ease

Advocacy is also easier than advice.

Reputations go to fearsome litigators. Movie adaptations go to those victorious in the courtroom. Client gratitude extends to winners.

So that an advisor can make a correct recommendation, an advisor must consider all the relevant facts and laws to make a correct prediction about likely legal outcomes.

2 MacEwen, Bruce. "The Future-Proof GC." Pinsent Masons. Accessed 6 October 2023. https://www.pinsentmasons.com/en-gb/thinking/brain-food/the-future-proof-gc. https://www.pinsentmasons.com/thinking/brain-food/the-future-proof-gc.

On the other hand, advocates need only concern themselves with evidence and theories most favourable to their clients. Inconvenient truths can be preliminarily ignored and, if not raised by the opponent, forever buried. Adopting a one-sided view of the world simplifies the advocate's role and keeps things easy.

Advice is also harder because it requires a lawyer to dispassionately balance competing arguments and *predict* how a court might decide. And, of course, predicting the future is tough, as difficult in law as any endeavour.

But for advocates, the need for difficult forecasts is avoided. The advocate must hammer home a parochial view favourable to the client and hope for the best. Intellectual balance and hard predictive calls are avoided, as is the ignominy of occasionally (and inevitably) being wrong.

Finally, advice is harder because it requires constant emotional vigilance.

From the moment the client walks in the door, it's natural to start (almost irrepressibly) sympathising with them. To see the world through their prism and lens, with all its distorting bias, and to begin empathising and aligning with their plight.

While this is an entirely human reaction, it is a natural tendency that must be *constantly fought* if the lawyer is to render proper advice. Partialism is fatal to objectivity, and with the loss of objectivity goes the ability to make an accurate assessment of whether the client should go to court — the very purpose of advice.

Hence, emotion and its stupefying influence must be constantly checked.

But easier said than done! It's very difficult to restrain these feelings from two perspectives. Firstly, interpersonal. We all want to be liked. However, adopting an admirable, fair-minded balance may be perceived by the client as a treasonous lack of intellectual loyalty to their cause. Or emotional detachment risks looking cold and uncaring.

Second, detachment is hard psychologically. The human mind is prejudiced towards believing its side of the argument is right.

In high school, I competed in the odd debating competition. I was generally agnostic when we were first presented with a topic and our side of the debate. '*Abortion? No strong views.*' However, after preparing arguments and practising furiously for days, by the time I came to speak in the debate, I was fundamentally and absolutely convinced of the correctness of my team's position and that it was the only view of the world a sensible person could contemplate ('*denying choice denies our humanity!*'). I had drunk the cool aid. I was emotionally committed to my position. While this *may* have enhanced my persuasiveness, it would have utterly sabotaged any ability to make a fair assessment of the objective merit of the same.

Many of us have fallen in love with our arguments in this way. This makes advising psychologically harder. We must take off the rosy goggles and constantly resist succumbing to passion and "our side is right" bias due to its corrupting influence on accuracy. Conversely, advocates don't have to perform the difficult task of holding back the emotional dam. Advocates can let go. Advocates *can* get emotionally overinvested. Advocates *should* empathise. They can subscribe to a worldview that aligns wholly with the client's interests, regardless of how divorced from reality it actually is. In fact, a certain preference for emotional loyalty over logical reality probably helps win cases.[3]

Overall favour to advocacy

Money. Glamour. Ease. For all these reasons, there is a general preference of lawyers to (again, subconsciously) prefer advocacy over advice.

To be clear, there is nothing inherently wrong with this. We all have to pursue our happiness, and if it's easier to be an advocate and the economic and professional incentives happen to be aligned that way, so be it. The world needs advocates. And following incentives is not immoral. That's the operating premise on which capitalism works.

However, it is legitimate to ask, from a macro-structural perspective, whether this tendency is causing unbalance in the profession as a whole.

---

3 MacEwen, Bruce. Tomorrowland: Scenarios for Law Firms Beyond the Horizon. Createspace Independent Publishing Platform, 2017.

The right balance?

If all patients committed to treatment without advice, what would we say? The treatment was ineffective? Inappropriate? Wasteful? Unfortunately, those descriptors can sometimes apply to litigation.

If all patients committed to treatment without advice, what would we say? The treatment was ineffective? Inappropriate? Wasteful?

When you have too many advocates and not enough advisors, you tend to end up with more litigation than necessary. If most lawyers operate in full-time advocate mode, what should be the last resort (court) becomes the first option. And while some cases do need judicial determination, others do not.

These latter cases clutter up the court system, jam the cogs, and divert energy and attention away from disputes that genuinely require a judicial decision. That's not a good result for society.

But this is the consequence of an excess of advocates. As warriors, they tend to charge into battle. Court is the default. Even if the odds are stacked against them, advocates get passionate about (and even cultivate the reputation for) being the underdog and not giving up without a '*hell of a fight*'. While such a view may be noble on the sports field and even an admired legal trait, it is likely to cloud independent thinking about other options.

Do we *have* to fight? *Can* we settle? *Should* we just go home? Without consideration of these questions, too many wrong cases inevitably go to court.

The best defence is recognition. It's fine to want to be a wonderful advocate. Still, it should also come with a clear-eyed realism that you are not always the best person to decide whether court is necessary *in the first place*.

Your emotion and zeal can come in *after* a client has made a rational decision to go to court.

The passion that makes you a great advocate in court must not be allowed to infect the client's rational preliminary consideration of whether to go to court at all.

Conclusion

Many lawyers want to identify themselves as being the best. But it begs the question. Best at what? A litigator can have two different jobs: advice and advocacy.

And while clients need both, it is the rare lawyer that achieves excellence in both. Divergent skills and (more importantly) divergent mindsets are required, and human beings, on the whole, are simply not that flexible nor capable of such split specialisation.

Forced to choose, many litigators gravitate towards advocacy. It's easier and results in more fame, glory and remuneration. For one lawyer, this is fine. But when everyone tends this way, it risks collective imbalance and professional drift and cluttering the courts unnecessarily with cases that would not have been there for want of a more dispassionate assessment.

After a spate of alcohol-fuelled violence between young men in Australia, advertising campaigns were run urging people to "think before they punch". It is sagacious advice. Before going to court, before committing to the punch, we should think: is this a good option? The only option? Given the costs of fighting, we must always consider the alternatives. Defaulting to a fight is not the mark of a reasoned strategy.

Defaulting to a fight is not the mark of a reasoned strategy.

There will always be a place for hot hearts. Passionate litigators who fight for their clients are a necessary part of an effectively functioning justice system.

But there is also a place for the cool head. And in some ways, the careful advisor who (when appropriate) advises against court does more for their client and the justice system as a whole than the famous litigator who fights every case to their dying breath.

Therefore, we must constantly check in with ourselves and, when working with the client, reflect on the following questions:

- What role am I currently in?
- Am I advising?
- Am I advocating?
- Is this what the client needs?
- (Importantly) Am I in the right frame of mind to do it?
- (Critically) Am I the best person to do it?

Without this, we risk disjuncture between what we are doing and the service the client really needs.

CHAPTER 2 - WHAT HAPPENED?

"We must trust to nothing but facts: These are presented to us by Nature, and cannot deceive."

- Antoine Lavoisie, French Chemist
(1743 – 1794)

"If you know the enemy and know yourself, you need not fear the result of a hundred battles. If you know yourself but not the enemy, for every victory gained you will also suffer a defeat. If you know neither the enemy nor yourself, you will succumb in every battle."

Sun Tzu, The Art of War

Whether advising or advocating, our first and most important job is determining "*what happened*".

In a small matter, the client can simply tell you. In large matters, we must piece the story together. This takes time. But it is an essential prerequisite to the rest of our jobs.

Until we know what happened, we cannot:

- Give legal advice. We cannot advise the client if we don't know what happened to them. We can only guess how the law will apply.
- Develop a litigation strategy. We cannot allocate resources without knowing the important issues. The only strategy possible is to "*gather more facts*".
- Estimate costs. We cannot predict the cost of proving an unknown. Instead, we can only update the client as costs are incurred.
- Ask for an expert opinion. If we cannot tell the expert what happened, we cannot get a sensible opinion in response.
- Recommend a settlement amount. Settlement requires balancing the costs and merits of litigation. Until we know what happened, we know neither.
- Accuse our opponent of wrongdoing. Any accusation is likely to lack detail or be wrong.
- Ask for justice from a decision-maker. Before justice is issued, the decision maker will say, "*first, tell me what happened*".

In summary, we must *first* determine what happened. Only then can we make sensible decisions about what to do about it.

Our Advantage

But if we know what happened, and our opponent does not, we have several advantages.

We can negotiate a favourable settlement. The seller knows the car's history and negotiates with a purchaser from a position of strength. Information is power. Should we desperately settle? Or can we be bullish?[4]

Information is power.

If we don't settle, we can plan for trial wisely. Knowing what happened means we can focus our resources on the important issues while our opponent stretches themselves thin across various issues, not knowing which are key.

We avoid waste. Suspicion comes readily in litigation. Any gaps in the story fill our minds with conspiracies about our opponent's actions and intentions, which, in turn, fuels a hunger for documents and information from our opponents. And while suspicion is understandable, it is rarely productive. But if we are confident in *what happened*, needless suspicion is allayed. Our client saves the costs of trying to pry documents from our opponents.

And suppose our opponent demands to inspect our documents. In that case, if we confidently know what happened, we know which to hand over willingly and which to ethically resist. Being selective conserves money and energy for more important issues.

In addition, our advocacy is more effective. A party that doesn't know (or like) what happened will prefer rhetoric over substance. Manifestations of outrage may appeal to clients keen to score points but are not very convincing. Simple statements of fact are usually better. Contrast the following:

---

4 Bruce Macewen, Tomorrowland: Scenarios for Law Firms Beyond the Horizon (Createspace Independent Pub, 2017)

Plaintiff

"On 16 December 2012, our client purchased a widget from the defendant's website. It should have been clear to any reasonable merchant that time was of the essence with the delivery of said widget. However, in contemptuous disregard for the plaintiff's consumer and moral rights, the defendant caused or otherwise bought into being a delay in the shipment of the said widget. The delay of two weeks in the package's arrival is unexplained and inexcusable. It was not only in breach of contract and the Vienna Convention on Contracts for the International Sale of Goods, but it was also so egregiously late that it casts into question the defendant's bona fides and their fitness to hold a licence to operate a widget business. The plaintiff seeks its full redress according to the law, including, inter alia, compensatory and punitive damages, non-pecuniary damages for emotional turmoil and legal costs on an indemnity basis."

Defendant

"On 16 December 2012, the plaintiff bought a widget on our website. Unfortunately, a postal strike in the plaintiff's country delayed delivery by two weeks. A postal employee is on standby to confirm this if necessary."

The old joke is that if the facts are against you, argue the law. But verbal eloquence and legality are a poor substitute for a clear understanding of "*what happened*". The plaintiff's legal team could not get to the bottom of this question. The defendant calmly presented what happened to the court and was more convincing. Good facts, like good ingredients, need little embellishment.

Good facts, like good ingredients, need little embellishment.

(Of course, there is some exaggeration in this example, but not much. The tone of the plaintiff's submissions is replicated in similar form across the legal world every day).

If we know what happened, we can make allegations against our opponents with precision. If we don't know, our allegations must be framed broadly (so as not to inadvertently preclude anything). But vague, broad and unsupported allegations are inflammatory, and the resulting mistrust mires litigation. Things that should be conceded become heated flashpoints. But suppose we know what happened and can allege it with specificity and proof. In that case, there is a better chance our opponents will sensibly capitulate to the point. This saves fuss.

Lastly, we can more accurately predict the cost of the litigation. Much cost uncertainty comes from not knowing what happened. How can you estimate the cost of proving an unknown? But once you know what happened, the next steps are easier to plan. The surprises are mainly gone. Your client can budget with greater confidence, relieving the unnecessary financial stress of blank cheque litigation.

(As a side note, it is probably futile to estimate the cost of *actually* uncovering "what happened". Investigations are uncertain. They proceed in spurts and splutters. They stall, and then a breakthrough is made. They are inherently unpredictable. The point is that once the investigation is complete and the story emerges, the remaining costs of litigating should ossify).

In summary, the more we know about what happened, the stronger our position. Omnipresence would render our advantage complete. While this is impossible (some witnesses are inaccurate, some documents will be missing or misleading, and some events vanish into history), there are good reasons to know more than our opponents about *what happened.*

Core Expertise

But in complex litigation, uncovering what happened is difficult. The story may be fragmented across hundreds of witnesses and millions of documents. No one person or document will know everything. Lawyers must, therefore, piece the story together, which requires good *investigation* skills.

Lawyers are professional sceptics, willing to assume nothing and demand proof. This is a good start. But investigations are not our core expertise.

Lawyers are professional sceptics, willing to assume nothing and demand proof. This is a good start. But investigations are not our core expertise. Journalists, historians, scientists and detectives are trained to uncover what happened. Law school asks us to *assume* what happened and apply the law. But we can improve.

First, we must embrace the task. Knowing what happened is the bedrock of everything we do. It can lack the glamour of the law. But it is paramount. We must treat it seriously.

Second, we must prioritise. Court deadlines and correspondence with our opponents capture a disproportionate amount of attention because there is urgent accountability to comply. But we must be disciplined to focus on the important (investigating), not just the pressing.

Third, we must expand our scope. We often hunt for evidence and examples to support an argument and discard the remainder. This may make us passable advocates. But without a complete picture of what happened, we cannot be good *advisors.*

Fourth, we must report accurately. This requires sticking to *facts.* We must not jump to conjecture or opinion. Analysis can follow once *what happened* is clear.

Other advice exists. But regardless of the tactics used, the overall objective remains. To properly advise our clients, we must first understand *exactly* what happened.

Getting better

On 14 August 2018, a section of the heavily trafficked Morandi bridge in northern Italy collapsed, tragically killing forty-three people. Once the shock and grief were allayed, there was a furious and unsurprising demand for answers. What happened? Who should find out? The attributes of the perfect investigator provide us with a good example to follow.

We would (of course) reject the company that built the bridge. It would be self-interested to exonerate itself. The investigators would be the judges in their own case. We would fear the report was biased. It would not be neutral, and it would not be trusted.

Self-evidently, good investigators must avoid bias. But bias has many guises. Lawyers often investigate only to support a pre-determined position, looking for evidence to help our argument and discarding the remainder. As mentioned above, this one-sided view of the world may make us passable advocates, and many of us are content or constrained to leave our role. However, without an unvarnished understanding of "*what happened*", we cannot be good *advisors*.

Bias has many guises.

We, therefore, need to be able to change gears. Ideally, we should dispassionately assess *all* the evidence to determine what happened. Only then should we consider switching to advocacy (noting the caution from Chapter 1 about the difficulty in successfully doing so).

When would we expect the investigation to start? Now! As with the bridge, the evidence goes cold, and unanswered questions howl louder with the passing of time. We must start quickly. Rubble must be immediately catalogued and preserved. Witnesses need locating and securing. Photographs must be taken.

The best tradition of legal fiction is for the truth to finally emerge at trial, at the crescendo of cross-examination (*"Did you order the Code Red? You're god damn right I did!"*). However, while this makes exciting literature, it is not diagnostic of good preparation. To be effective, we need to know the facts sooner. We should therefore start as soon as possible.

Would we expect the investigators to do everything? Probably not! Specialists would help. A construction company would clear and catalogue the rubble. Forensic photographers would capture visual evidence of the collapsed section. Private investigators would collect statements from witnesses. Engineers would examine fractures. The investigator in charge would manage the effort and author the final report. Investigating the bridge's collapse, as in its construction, would be achieved with intelligent subcontracting.

Investigating the bridge's collapse, as in its construction, would be achieved with intelligent subcontracting.

Lawyers tend to horde all investigative responsibility. Why? Inertia partially explains – it's always been so, and nervous clients may prefer orthodoxy. Two, lawyers tend not to accept evidence we have not seen, making relying on others to perform any investigations difficult. Three, lawyers' investigations will be privileged and helpful if the client's story is unflattering.

The drawback is that lawyers are not trained investigators. Bright and diligent certainly, but untrained. Where appropriate, we could look for opportunities to subcontract to specialists. There is nothing inherent in investigations that especially qualifies lawyers to perform them. Scientists, detectives and journalists perform similar tasks daily. This opens a field of possibilities regarding how the work could be performed.

Would we expect our investigators to be serious about investigating? Yes!

We would want them to be thorough, engaged and eager to investigate. After all, judgements will be made on the outcome of the investigation. It needs to be right.

Many lawyers like to execute litigation tactics or debate the law. Uncovering what happened is not always considered as interesting. But if we are to retain responsibility for investigating, we should do it with the same gusto. It is important and deserves the same energy as we approach law and tactics.

Would we expect the investigators to be trained? Yes! We would expect competence in capturing, organising and sharing facts. We would expect specialised tools and methodologies. We would not accept general intelligence as a substitute for specific knowledge.

Lawyers would benefit from training in investigative techniques and tools. Such training is uncommon. But if we accept Drucker's[5] observation that brightness is not a substitute for skill, we should make an effort to seek it out.

Making it easier

In complex litigation, investigations are time-consuming. But small things can help.

Investigations are easier if the information is organised. It is easier to reassemble the bridge if we (a) know what the original looked like, (b) have preserved all the rubble, and (c) are confident nothing key is missing. This makes preserving and organising evidence – to the extent our client has not – an important upfront investment.

Investigations are also easier if we focus. It is easy to investigate only in support of other activities – legal analysis, advocacy preparation – and not privilege investigations as important stand-alone activities. But so conducted, investigations become sporadic and haphazard rather than planned and methodical. This unnecessarily inhibits effectiveness.

5 Drucker, Peter F. Managing Oneself. Harvard Business Press, 2008.

Knowing enough

Would we want the investigators to sort rubble for a decade? No! We need answers sooner.

Because it is important, and there is always more to discover about the past, trying to figure out what happened can be a never-ending task.

Of course, figuring out what happened is a critical first step. But there are *other* steps we must get to as well. Like all good things, we need to know when we've had enough.

If we never have the courage to say, "*we know enough*", the client does not receive settled legal advice. It can also sap the energy of the lawyers – like penal labour, a never-ending task is demotivating. And it stunts a lawyer's development as a *law*yer, as the law is never considered.

We must be courageous to stop early enough to consider other issues before trial – advice, strategy, settlement – from a settled factual position.

Of course, we must be *complete* in our investigations, or they lose credibility. But we must be *courageous* to stop early enough to consider other issues before trial – advice, strategy, settlement – from a settled factual position.

Conclusion

When bad things happen, there is a natural human desire for answers. What happened? How could this have happened? For public disasters or crimes, public bodies usually investigate. Only once the conclusions have been reached do the lawyers become involved.

In the private realm, when something goes wrong ('*we have lost a lot of money*'), lawyers are looked to for both answers – what happened, and what should we do? Clients, therefore, need good *investigators* as much as they need good lawyers. As in medicine, accurate diagnosis is half the cure.

Investigative skill receives little focus at law school, in continuing education, or when marketing ourselves to clients. However, it is foundational to our role. Without knowing what happened, we are merely swept along, with the client, in the current of where the case takes us, bemoaning the uncertainty of litigation. We cannot chart a course.

CHAPTER 3 - TYPES OF DISPUTES

"The study of taxonomy in its broadest sense is probably the oldest branch of biology or natural history as well as the basis for all the other branches, since the first step in obtaining any knowledge of things about us is to discriminate between them and to learn to recognize them."

Richard E. Blackwelder (1909 – 2001)

In the taxonomy of litigation, there are three types of disputes.

Factual

Factual disputes concern what happened. For instance:

- You shot him! I did not!
- You agreed! No way!
- I did not have sexual relations with that woman. You did!

To resolve these disputes, parties present their version of events to the decision-maker. The decision maker hears witnesses, watches cross-examination and reads documents. Ultimately, they decide whom to *believe*.

Factual disputes are quests for truth, not legal debates. Deciding whom to believe is an exercise in common sense. Once done, the legal conclusion is often obvious (after all, if the defendant wasn't there, they're not guilty). This means ordinary people can decide factual disputes, with juries the quintessential example.

Being believed requires evidence, so lawyers must be good at finding and presenting it. They must be good storytellers. Legal mastery is less important, as while the law is never irrelevant, command of legal principles is secondary to the ability to tell a convincing tale (*"Here are the six reasons you should believe my client was not involved"*).

Factual disputes are hard on clients from at least two perspectives. There is the time cost. Clients must heavily assist with preparation as they are the primary source of the evidence necessary to win. And there is also the psychological cost. As the parties disagree about what happened, they are implicitly (and often explicitly) calling each other liars. This is upsetting, and the trauma can linger.

Factual disputes are also hard on the court system – they are tough to settle and, therefore, occupy significant court time. Settlement can be elusive because when litigants become upset, they often become intransigent, entrenched and embittered. So even if the lawyers can agree on a fair settlement sum, the litigants themselves might sabotage any deal because of an unwillingness to back down.

Even if the lawyers can agree on a fair settlement sum, the litigants themselves might sabotage any deal because of an unwillingness to back down.

Moreover, factual disputes are common. People readily disagree about what happened when it is in their interest. They also take time. Preparing and presenting evidence from multiple witnesses is time-consuming. Hearings take weeks or months, not hours or days, and are unpredictable as the story's drama unfolds. As lawyers charge hourly, factual disputes are commensurately expensive. Factual disputes are, therefore, a significant fiscal and temporal burden on the judicial system.

What of appeals? Rare. Appeal courts cannot decide whom to believe without re-hearing the evidence themselves. Only clear error warrants intervention.

Standard Disputes

Standard disputes ask whether the behaviour was *reasonable*. Such tests and similar variations are common.

For instance:

- You were *careless*! I was not!
- That homicide was *justified*! No chance!
- You didn't use your *best endeavours*. I did!

These are not disputes about what happened. They are disputes about agreed facts that are *characterised*.

Parties will present arguments about why the conduct did or didn't meet the standard. The decision-maker balances the arguments and makes the (often instinctive) call. In doing so, they are supposed to channel the collective wisdom of society. This common sense but representative task is again well suited to juries.

Standard disputes are also common. The law has many objective and vague standards (i.e. *reasonable person, all necessary steps, best endeavours*). The vagueness is necessary to give the law flexibility to deal with different scenarios. But it also encourages disagreement.

To win these cases, lawyers must convincingly explain why society should or should not condone certain behaviour. Most effectively, this takes thinking about the behaviour broadly. Will insurance premiums rise? Will people drive recklessly on the roads?

Standards disputes are easier on clients. The facts are agreed upon, so they don't need to help gather evidence. And while no one likes to be accused of being negligent (or similar), litigants are likely to privately acknowledge there could be differing views. This cools tensions, encouraging settlement.

Cases that don't settle usually finish quickly. As what happened is agreed, witnesses are unnecessary. Even in cases with experts (to explain whether a *professional* standard was met), a trial about behaviour characterisation will be brief. Not coincidentally, this makes standard disputes cheaper than their factual counterparts.

But appeals are still rare. The tests are common sense ones. Appeal judges have no more authority to decide whether a standard was met.

Appeal judges have no more authority to decide whether a standard was met.

Legal Disputes

Finally, legal disputes ask how the *law* applies to what happened. For instance:

- Are waiters' tips subject to income tax?
- Does an advertisement create a legally binding promise?
- Are private parking fines enforceable?

In the common law world, decision-makers resolve disputes by analogy. How have similar cases in the past been resolved?

Lawyers will submit why particular past cases (favourable to their client) are appropriate analogies (or *precedents*). They may also suggest that certain legislation or contract terms are applicable. Reconciling these submissions requires legal training, meaning judges (and only judges) should decide on legal disputes.

Lawyers like legal disputes. It is our comfort zone. We study the rules and how they apply. But somewhat ironically, legal disputes are the rarest type.

To win legal disputes, lawyers need knowledge of cases accumulated through study and experience. Selecting a helpful case, they argue it is a suitable precedent. Knowledge is less helpful than creativity in novel disputes (like about unique contracts). But regardless, these are intellectual debates, and legal smarts are non-negotiables.

Being disputes about the *law*, clients cannot contribute to the preparation and are relegated to being (financially) interested observers.

These dry academic debates will rarely be emotional. This theoretically should help settlement. But as legal disputes often emerge only after the facts settle, sunk legal costs can be a psychological barrier against this[6]. (The *"I've come too far to settle now"* mentality).

Hearings are quick. Days at most. But the cost remains high. Short presentations belie long preparation, and the legal scholars required to win are rare, in demand, and (hence) expensive.

And appeals? More common. Senior judges are well qualified to check the legal conclusions of lower courts. And as legal decisions form new precedents, there is a public utility in scrutinising the correctness of decisions.

Complexity

Above is a clear trichotomy: factual, standard and legal. Alas, the real world is more complex.

Some (apparent) disputes are not. Coaxing money from a disinclined debtor can require a lawyer, the court and the weight of the law, but unless the defence is more sophisticated than "*I'd rather not pay*", there is no dispute.

---

6 John Celona, Winning at Litigation through Decision Analysis: Creating and Executing Winning Strategies in any Litigation or Dispute (Springer, 2016).

Alas, the real world is more complex.

Also unhelpful to taxonomy – disputes *mutate.* Many are born as simple creatures (*"you negligently ran a red light and injured me"*). Then distractions multiply. The defendant replies:

- *"prove I own a car";*
- *"prove I was driving that day";*
- *"in any case, you hurt yourself playing football";*
- *"and you are not that badly injured,"*

Adding:

- *"plus, you were drunk";*
- *"and I was out of my mind!"*[7]

The real dispute (*"what colour was the light?"*) is obscured by the proliferation of arguments.

This happens because (a) erecting arguments is cheap – just pen to paper; and (b) throwing lots of darts increases the chances of a hit. Contrast the military, where attacks are expensive and discrimination necessary.

Moreover, the line between standard and legal disputes can be hazy. Both concern the meaning of words. But is a word (like *"dishonest"*) a common sense word applicable to a jury? Or a word with a careful legal meaning, defined by years of preceding cases? Regularly unclear, it makes categorisation controversial (though the fact the border is disputed should not stop us from recognising two countries exist).

7 With thanks again to the inimitable Irving Younger and his "insane goat" anecdote.

Why should we care about categorisation?

Several reasons.

Society can allocate decision-makers. Otherwise, we risk inefficiency (if an overqualified judge must use common sense) or failure (if an unqualified jury decides legal issues). Neither is good.

More selfishly for lawyers, it assists in preparation. Recognising each dispute requires a different outcome (i.e. believe me, condone my behaviour or adopt my legal analysis) facilitates sensible planning.

While we cannot guarantee outcomes, understanding what's disputed facilitates sensible predictions.

Clients will be prepared. While we cannot guarantee outcomes, understanding what's disputed facilitates sensible *predictions*. Legal disputes are readily appealed. Factual disputes take time. Standards disputes can be settled. Clients are forewarned rather than simply told: "*litigation is unpredictable*".

Clients can also pick a lawyer. The skills required for each case are different. Do you need a legal technician? Or a good storyteller? A mix? By knowing what type of dispute they have, the client will be armed with the right questions.

Finally, courts can deploy the right tools. For instance, discovery is the most expensive step of modern litigation. But if the dispute is not factual, courts may skip it.

Eye on the prize

Correct characterisation also brings focus. Standard and legal disputes often deteriorate into factual disputes as defendants reflexively deny all facts of a claim.

This happens for two reasons.

- First, the defendant might be unclear about what happened. When you don't know, it's safer to deny.
- Second, denying facts is the easiest defence. "I asked you to wash the dishes". 'No, you didn't!". It requires no law degree nor any real imagination. It's very accessible.

So, it's common for defendants to deny facts almost reflexively. But it's also a wasteful tendency.

Consider this example:

Tax agency: Those tips you received are taxable.
Waiter / Defendant: What tips?

The flat denial requires the court to resolve a factual dispute ("*did the waiter earn any tips?*") before the legal dispute ("*are tips taxable?*") is considered. And as it is a factual dispute, it will take time and expense. It may, from mutual accusations of dishonesty, become heated. Of course, sometimes, making a factual defence and starting a factual dispute is appropriate, but this warrants a careful and deliberate choice – not basal instinct.

This is not to deny anyone a defence. But understanding what's in dispute (facts, standards or the law) equips the court to probe and test. Do you *really* deny receiving the tips? Or is this really a legal dispute about the taxation of your tips?

Identifying the real dispute avoids wasting time on peripheral issues.

Avoiding disputes

Further, knowing what *causes* disputes helps avoid them.

Documenting everything prevents factual disputes. People rarely argue with records. Conversely, factual disputes without verifying evidence must be resolved in court – denial is otherwise too easy.

People rarely argue with records.

Standards disputes can be eliminated by mandating *specific* rather than reasonable actions. But there are costs. We lose flexibility and give lawbreakers a clear target to work around. Where the balance lies is a question for society and its lawmakers.

Keeping the law simple and stable stops legal disputes. Uncertainty created by new laws or bespoke contracts invites disagreement.

Conclusion

No two disputes are the same. However, many are similar. And by observing and extracting what makes disputes similar, we gain some helpful insights.

Lawyers often describe disputes as "*criminal*", "*commercial*", "*environmental*", "*personal injury*", or similar. This provides a setting but not a strategy. It is more helpful to ask what's in dispute. Facts? Standards? Or the law?

And it is important we do. Because if our opponents recognise the type of dispute and prepare accordingly, even the smartest lawyer risks being defeated by overwhelming focus.

Every day, across the world, there are millions of disputes, but only three types. The key question is: which do *you* have?

CHAPTER 4 - VALUING, IMPROVING AND CONVEYANCING

"If it doesn't add value, it's waste".

Henry Ford (1863 - 1947)

Selling land for maximum profit requires three steps.

1. Valuing the land;
2. Improving the land; and
3. Conveying the land to the new owner for cash.

Running litigation for a maximum return requires the same three steps.

Valuation

When deciding whether to sell, an owner will first want to know the value of the land. What they are sitting on. How much it's worth?

To assist, a professional valuer will review the land's unique features and, combining these observations with their professional experience, assess the land's current "*as is*" value. From this, the owner can decide what they want to do. Sit on or sell?

Litigation is the same. From the moment it is born, every lawsuit has an intrinsic "*as is*" value. This valuation arises simply because of the circumstance in which the case was born. How and when the money was taken. Who said what to whom? When and why the bridge collapsed.

The moment these legally significant events occur, the unimproved value of the case springs to life and remains static, frozen in time. The role of the legal advisor, as with the valuer, is to review the unique features of the case (the facts) and, amalgamating that with their knowledge of the law, indicate the value of the lawsuit. From this, the client can decide whether they wish to proceed to litigation.

A valuer normally expresses their opinion numerically, whereas lawyers usually prefer narrative descriptions ("a good chance of winning a million dollars"). But don't let the intervention of the alphabet fool you – the lawyer is still providing a monetary valuation.

Valuing a house is usually quite straightforward, whereas valuing litigation can be a little erratic – the value of the case will fluctuate with the state of the known facts at the time. And as the facts often unravel slowly, the valuation can jump around a bit as different pieces of information are discovered. But eventually, as the number of "unknowns" reduces and a full picture of the case emerges, the true valuation of the case will stabilise.

Improving

Upon receiving the valuation, the owner decides to sell. Of course, they can go to market "as is". But most rational owners, seeking to maximise profits, will aim to improve the value of the land in the eyes of the marketplace.

They mow the lawn, fix the gutters and replace the shower. Cut the hedge, paint the door and upgrade the climate control. Tinker, tailor and trim. Invest for a return.

Such home improvements are also possible for our lawsuit. While physical manipulation of an intangible asset is not possible, there are other things lawyers can do. This, primarily, is improving the arguments supporting the case with creativity and practising and refining those arguments until they are perfected.

This requires, among other things, sitting quietly and *thinking*. Whilst by definition nebulous, it's critical to improving case value. A case backed by thoughtful, insightful and creative arguments is more likely to prevail and, hence, be more valuable than a case without them.

A case backed by thoughtful, insightful and creative arguments is more likely to prevail and, hence, be more valuable than a case without them.

Conveyancing

Once the asset is valued and improved, it's time to monetise the latent value by exchanging it for cash. In real estate, this is the legal process of conveying the land to a new owner for the purchase price.

While conveyancing is necessary for the value of the property to be converted into cash, it does not *increase* the value of the property.

A lawsuit, too, has its conveyancing aspects. Once the value of the case is identified and improved to the greatest extent possible, it needs to be monetised. It must be taken to court. The courtroom is to the lawsuit as the conveyancer's office is to the land – in both instances, it is the process by which the asset is converted to cash.

As with actual conveyancing, when monetising in court, there are several required steps:

- **Setting it up:** This requires filing the lawsuit with a court and negotiating with the decision maker and your opponents how the lawsuit will be run.

- **Obtain the supporting material:** Lawyers must prepare supporting material for the case, usually a trifecta of witness statements, expert reports and legal submissions.
- **Manage the effort:** All litigation is a project, and the above steps must be project-managed to ensure they are done on time, on budget and to the required quality.
- **Present the case in court:** Finally, standing up and making the case orally in court.

All these steps are required to convert the potential value of the litigation into actual cash. If the lawsuit is not filed, evidence is not prepared, deadlines are missed, or the presentation of the case is fumbled, the suit will be lost, and the plaintiff will receive nothing.

But critically, as with all conveyancing steps, these steps do nothing to *improve* the case's value. This is an important observation, so it warrants further discussion.

Setting it up

First, consider "*setting it up*". This step kicks off the lawsuit process and establishes the framework of the trial. It starts with the right form. What needs to be filed? Where? Is there a fee? And so on – such trifles are important and often not trifles at all.

Once the case is "in" the system (whether that's a court, an arbitration, a binding conciliation or otherwise) comes the negotiation. Where will we hold the trial? Who will be the decision maker? What witnesses will appear? In what order? How long will it take? What rules of evidence apply? The potential list of issues to be resolved can be lengthy.

Resolving these questions can require extensive discussion between litigants and the decision-making body, especially if the body is being established for the first time (arbitration, a royal commission, or a board of inquiry). Discussions are ongoing, and answers are expected so that these negotiations can occupy lots of attention.

But resolving these questions is the equivalent of deciding what neutral stadium will host the soccer game, who will wear the white shorts, and what colour the corner flags will be. Necessary details, but hardly the main game, and not capable of making a fundamental difference in our chance of winning.

Necessary details, but hardly the main game, and not capable of making a fundamental difference in our chance of winning.

"*Setting it up*" is, therefore, a conveyancing activity. Necessary to monetise the case because the case needs a properly established forum, but it makes little difference to the value. You need to do it to avoid losing (because without "setting it up", there is no trial, and the plaintiff gets nothing), but it doesn't help you win.

Obtain the supporting material

Consider also "*obtaining supporting material*". These are the necessary documents, submissions and testimony that support your legal argument.

Of course, there is no doubt such material is necessary. Without supporting material, tangible evidence, submissions and reports, even the most valuable case will be quickly thrown out of court. In our justice system, the onus is on the parties to present evidence and arguments to support their claim. No documents mean no case.

However, as indispensable as they are to support our argument, the supporting materials are *not* the arguments themselves. They are simply the necessary physical manifestation of the ideas and arguments that have been conceived earlier in the "*improvement*" stage. For instance, if in the "*improvement*" stage, we come up with an excellent argument in support of our case, in the "*conveyancing*" stage, we bring this argument to life by obtaining the necessary witness statement, legal submissions and expert evidence. But in doing these things, we simply realise the value of the argument already concocted – we are not adding to the case's value. The architect has already invented the argument. Obtaining the supporting material is simply applying the steel, nuts and bolts.

The river of supporting material can never rise above its source. The argument is what wins the case. The supporting material is just the supporting rivets.

Therefore, while gathering supporting material is necessary to ensure the case is not immediately dismissed, it does nothing to *improve* the value of the case. It prevents losing but doesn't help you win. It is, hence, a conveyancing activity only.

Managing the effort

Third, consider "*managing the effort*". Again, it is undoubtedly necessary to properly monetise the case. Litigation, especially large and complex litigation, is a project and must be professionally managed as such. Resources, time and people need to be combined to "set the case up" and "gather the necessary supporting material", with everyone arriving with everything prepared on the trial date.

For those who have had the privilege, it's like planning a wedding. It's a lengthy process of multiple work streams with different time frames, all galvanising together for a large, significant, important date at the end of the year. As the big day approached, there was a last-minute surge of organisation activity because the alternative – no flowers, no music or the mother of the bride not having a place to stay – was a disastrous alternative.

Therefore, project management in litigation, as with weddings (which hopefully don't occur sequentially), requires a significant amount of attention. The consequences of missing a deadline, a witness not arriving from the airport on time for their testimony or lacking any material to support an argument (because it was overlooked in the flurry of activity) can be fatal to any case.

Project management seeks to avoid this by ensuring all the boxes are ticked on the way to the big day. It plays an important role in ensuring the case is not lost.

But for the third time, that is the outer edge of what project management can achieve. It can avoid suddenly devaluing the case (by it being lost). Still, you are unlikely ever to "manage" your way into improving the case's value. Ticking the boxes simply avoids undercutting the intrinsic value of the case. It avoids losing but doesn't help to win.

Presenting the case in court

Finally, consider *"presenting the case in court"*. I consider this (somewhat surprisingly, perhaps) to be an administrative conveyancing step as well.

It is a truism that cases, like World Cups, are won in the preparation. They can certainly be lost on game day, but they are never *won* on game day. Lawsuits, soccer games and gold medals are *won* (despite fictional portrayals to the contrary) in the long slog of hard preparation that occurs, unseen, in the backroom before the glamour of the big event.

The athlete may be overawed by the situation and stumble at the final hurdle. The best soccer player in the world may succumb to pressure and miss the winning penalty. The greatest litigator may misstep in the courtroom with a tactical error ("*Mr Simpson, please try on the glove for the jury*"). These are all instances of errors that destroy any chance of victory and are examples of *losing* when it matters most.

However, the inverse is impossible. Regardless of how talented and persuasive an advocate you are, you can never overcome a lack of preparation to win an otherwise lost case. That is why they say that "*preparation is the mark of a professional*". Without it, you are nothing.

And because of this, the fact that cases can be lost at trial but are never won at trial, I relegate the actual presentation of the case to conveyancing status.

Necessary not to lose? Yes. Must be handled competently? Absolutely. But can it help improve the chances of winning? Never.

Analysis

If we accept this analysis, we can see that valuation identifies value, and conveyancing monetises it. Still, only the "*improvement*" step actually increases the asset's value.

From this framework, an outside observer might rationally conclude the lawyers:

- proceed through each step of valuing, improving and conveyancing sequentially, and
- spend the majority of their time in the "*improvement*" stage.

However, this expectation rarely aligns with reality.

Problem 1: Skipping valuing, jumping immediately to improving

The first problem is to be seduced by the "sexy" act of improving, wishing to start on it immediately without laying the groundwork of a proper valuation.

Such eagerness is understandable but a false economy. You cannot improve the property if you haven't first identified its underlying value. You need to know where you are starting from and any limitations before trying and improving.

Suppose a property owner rushed in and tried to make home improvements before properly valuing the land and understanding all its subtleties. In that case, they'd likely hit a litany of problems. Perhaps the amazing proposed extension is actually unfeasible because it breaches planning regulations. Maybe the wonderfully planned flowerbed is pointless as there is lead in the ground. Possibly installing that charming lattice would be an utter waste as the airport will acquire the land compulsorily to build a runway. The lack of underlying information about the land confounds your attempts at improving it.

For the same reasons, it is equally pointless trying to "improve" the lawsuit without a clear understanding of its underlying features and constraints (in other words, its "intrinsic value").

You need to understand the underlying facts in order to be able to launch into creative thinking of arguments. Otherwise, we are inevitably confronted by a lack of information. The dialogue runs: "*Why don't we argue this*?" the counter comes, "*Do the facts support it*?" and the slinking response is ", *Not sure, I'll have to check*".

Avoid wasted energy. Before launching the new garden or extension, know the lead levels and planning regulations. And before launching into the creative construction of arguments, know the facts of the case.

Problem 2: Skipping valuing and improving

The second problem occurs when lawyers skip steps one ("valuing") and two ("improving") entirely.

Something happens to the client, and instead of providing a valuation of their case and attempting to improve it through creatively thinking of arguments, the lawyer immediately seeks to monetise it by filing in court.

Such a step may be premature if the case is worthless, or alternatively, if the case does have some value, we are leaving money on the table by failing to try and improve it before closing the sale.

Skipping steps is usually symptomatic of a (1) busy (2) advocate. As advocates, they tend to dive immediately into running a case without first considering or advising whether the case has any value. And being *busy*, they often lack time to sit back and quietly consider how the intrinsic value of the case can be improved.

In this, they may be a victim of their prior success. Busy lawyers have multiple pulls on their time. This means they may readily throw their client's case "into the system", but with so many clients, they simply lack the time to properly assess the value of, or seek to improve, the value of the case.

Of course, failing to do any due diligence about the value of the case risks clogging the courts with worthless claims and wasting the plaintiff's time. And by failing to improve the case, we do a disservice to our client. Yet, this is a common problem for busy advocates.

Problem 3: Skipping improvements

Even for lawyers with the luxury of more time, another common problem is skipping the "*improvement*" step because of the pressing demands of valuation and conveyancing.

Investigating forever

The first part of this problem is getting stuck in valuation mode.

A proper valuation of the case inevitably requires a complete understanding of "*what happened*". This usually requires *investigations*. In furtherance of this, we dredge through reams of documents, speak to endless witnesses and try and pry as much information from the clutches of the other side as we can through discovery.

To properly value a case, this is all good and important work. The more we know, the greater our power. However, we should not be lured into thinking this does anything to *increase* the chance of winning the case. The facts, notwithstanding their importance to the valuation of the case, like gravity, are set. The events have happened. The story coalesced. The facts are fixed. At best, as you investigate facts, they, like archaeological ruins, can be *uncovered* but never altered or improved.

If you uncover favourable facts, do not trick yourself into thinking *you* have added value to the case. The facts were always that way. You have not changed them. You have simply found them.

Therefore, despite the fundamental importance of understanding "what happened", if we are seeking to *add* value to the client's case (and not simply uncover and identify what the natural value is), we must, at some point, move on from investigating the case to actually improving it. To going: now that we know the facts, what will we say? To create new and fresh arguments.

That, after all, is the entire point of preparation – to arrive at court with something interesting to say, not simply (except in the rarest instances) present the facts as you have found them.

Valuation is the launching pad for improvement. Of course, it must be done solidly, but we can't neglect actually launching as well.

Lost in the conveyancing weeds

The second part of the problem is getting lost in the conveyancing weeds.

Focusing on conveyancing is tempting because of the short-term catastrophic consequences if you don't. You lose if you fail to file the form, neglect drafting the document, or miss the deadline. Instantly. This naturally induces anxiety and attention. Suppose you are walking along a narrow ledge above a precipice. In that case, it is understandable to remain focused on the short-term tasks immediately in front of you (one foot after the other) rather than on the bigger picture strategic question of whether this ledge is the right, best or most appropriate one to be shimmying along.

Yet this conveyancing work is not where the most value is delivered. Necessary? Yes. Must be competently performed? Yes. But able to improve the value of the case? No.

Conveyancing is simply the process of shepherding the case through the necessary procedural steps in an attempt to monetise its intrinsic value. While the shepherd never wants to lose his sheep, regardless of how well he performs his role, the shepherd does not increase the intrinsic value of the sheep. He is simply responsible for ensuring they arrive safely at the market. The quality of the flock's breeding, upbringing and care will determine whether they obtain a high price for their wool. The most the shepherd can do is ensure the flock does not wander off and get (along with any potential profits) lost.

And this is what the conveyancer does – ensure the case's value is not lost. They have a necessary functionary role in helping the value of the asset be monetised but do not in and of themselves do anything to improve the asset's value.

The real magicians are those who can find a way to *improve* the value of an asset. I say this because this is where the *magic* is. We can see this through salary data. As necessary as they are, valuers and conveyancers are rarely among the financial elite of society. They are careful professions fulfilling a necessary function but do not provide great leaps in the land's value. However, successful property developers who take the land as a raw resource and improve it before monetising tend to be among the wealthiest individuals in the world. And it is not an accident. These induvial are not merely identifying the value of the land or performing the necessary steps to monetise it; they are actually *generating* value. It's appropriate that they keep a proportion of the additional value they generate.

The conveyancing aspect often takes significant time, energy, and effort and creates much stress. Avoiding a misstep that can cause you to lose is stressful - that ledge is high. The sheep are sheep and constantly follow each other into a potential disaster. Yet this constant anxiety with shepherding the case through the necessary procedural steps ties up a significant amount of mental attention, often to the detriment of actually *improving* the case.

Conclusion –A better balance

As litigation lawyers, we have many tasks on our plate and to-do lists. But in the interest of being more effective and of more value to our clients, it behoves us to place each of these items through the following prism: is this action part of a valuation, improvement or conveyance?

This is an idealised model, and we cannot always segregate these steps neatly and sequentially – real life can intervene. But it remains a useful mental guide, regardless of whether the actual order of activities shows strict fidelity to the ideal.

Without considering this model, the gravitational pull of our work will inevitably cause us to drift away from *improving* and get bogged down in *valuing* and *conveyancing.*

If you fail to take time to think, no one will know except you.

Why do I say this? Simple. In addition to the points above, valuing and conveyancing naturally lead to tasks – deadlines and deliverables. Therefore, it is probably a fair bet that the majority of things on our to-do lists at any one time consist of activities supporting conveyancing and valuation only.

Of course, let there be no mistake; these activities cannot be ignored. But we must not fall into the trap of believing that identifying the land's intrinsic value or filling in the necessary forms to sell it is where the real value is rendered. The real value to the client occurs (or should occur) a step earlier, in the improvement stage.

But as this "improvement" work often consists of quietly thinking about the case in an effort to identify creative arguments, it is rarely on a to-do list and, even more problematically, rarely has a deadline. If you fail to write a piece of advice, your client will follow you up. If you fail to file a form with the court, sirens go off, and it's panic stations. Yet if you fail to take time to think, no one will know except you.

In attempting to maximise the value of our client's case, we, therefore, must display significant self-discipline to not simply attend to the urgent and pressing valuing and conveyancing work but make sure, before we try and sell the house, that we have done everything necessary proceeding that to scrub it to its most attractive and valuable level.

A good litmus test is this. If you are *doing* anything, you are either identifying the case's value or holding it level pending monetisation. Only *thinking* (that is, of new and compelling arguments) drives the value upwards. As we look down our tasks list, and the things we have done with our busy day, that's a profound thought.

To be more effective, this is our challenge. To avoid relentless activity driving out actually improving the value of the case. To avoid simply uncovering the intrinsic value of the case and shepherding it to market. But to actually improve it.

Because inevitably, the litigation lawyers who deliver the most value to their clients work hardest at *improving* the value of their lawsuit – not simply valuing or conveying it.

CHAPTER 5 - CREATIVITY

"Imagination is more important than knowledge."

Albert Einstein (1879 – 1955)

How do we do it, then? How do we *improve* the value of the case? As briefly mentioned, principally, it is by coming up with creative arguments.

The power of creativity

Let's review an example of the power of creativity.

A homeless person steals a blanket to sleep in during winter. The police arrest them and prosecute the matter in court. While the law on stealing is clear, the jury's impressionistic sympathy will lie with the poor, Olivier Twist-type thief.

How does it play out? The defendant's lawyer adopts a fairly obvious position:

> *You have heard from the defendant, and their testimony is uncontested: they had to steal the blanket to stay warm on a cold night because, owing to their destitution, they could not afford to purchase it.*

What sort of society could convict this person, a vulnerable member of society, in this situation? Members of the jury, your conscience and sympathies must revolt.

The prosecution has the letter of the law on their side. Still, it has an uphill battle to overcome the almost irresistible desire to be merciful to this poor thief. What to do? Think laterally. Instead of just relying on the letter of the law and admitted facts, they imbue some creativity into their argument to improve it – see if you are convinced:

Whilst our hearts feel nothing but sympathy for the defendant's unfortunate position, you, as sworn members of the jury, are entrusted to apply the law dispassionately without fear or favour. Conscience and sympathy do not come into it.

And in any case, speaking of sympathies, whilst the defendant alleges they avoided an evil by taking the blanket to stay warm, there is an unanswered question: what about the greater evil perpetuated on society that the stealing represents?

What about the small business owner, who is not represented here without an eloquent lawyer to present their case, from whom the blanket was taken? Are they not also entitled to our sympathy? You members of the jury: have you not had something taken from you? A bike, perhaps, as a child? A cherished possession? A loved one? Is that hollow feeling of violation not familiar to you? And what of the deprivation of that portion of the shopkeeper's income? Will the shopkeeper struggle to make ends meet now? Could they sustain a business that was constantly stolen from? The answer is, of course, no.

But that is what we encourage when we excuse stealing. Feelings of violation, shops closing, and further poverty spreading. The reality, members of the jury, is that by acquitting the defendant based on their poverty, we merely perpetuate greater poverty throughout our entire society. This is not a situation that I, nor, I implore you, could tolerate.

Who wins? I do not intend to lead the jury, but the prosecution's closing must at least partially persuade our verdict. A staid recitation of "*the law says you cannot steal*" would probably be unconvincing. However, the creative reference to the greater evil of permitting stealing and spreading poverty should at least make the jury pause. I leave you to your deliberations.

Whatever your verdict, we can draw this clear conclusion: creativity has improved the prosecution's argument, as it does with all arguments. A bland recitation of the law and the facts gets only a passing grade and will always be trumped by the argument that takes these building blocks and adds a layer of inspiration, spark and insight.

A bland recitation of the law and the facts gets only a passing grade and will always be trumped by the argument that takes these building blocks and adds a layer of inspiration, spark and insight.

Creative lawyers?

Therefore, the recommendation for better arguments is to be "*more creative*". As an idea, this is a bit edgy. Many lawyers view "*creativity*" (and its variants) with some suspicion.

We are a conservative, backwards-facing profession built on traditions and precedents. Our time horizon backward can extend to centuries, whilst our time horizon forward tends not to extend far past our next deadline or end of the financial year. Slow, careful and cautious? Yes. But fresh, new and inspired? These are not the words that come to mind when describing our collective mindset.

A small handful of lawyers may eagerly embrace the call to be creative. Then, I suspect, there will be the silent majority who will probably initially dismiss the call for creativity as an instance of some naive or benign misguidance. This reluctance stems from an inherent resistance to progress. As Jim Hacker says in Yes Minister: *"You don't understand. It's not a compliment. Creative and imaginative are two of Humphry's most damming criticisms"*.

Indispensable need

But regardless of our personal view (or prejudice), the reality is that litigators cannot do without creativity if they wish to be successful in court.

As we saw above, creativity improves arguments. But even more fundamentally, regardless of the dispute, every case not only should have but actually *needs* creativity. Successful arguments cannot be recycled from case to case; they must be *created* for each case we tackle.

We will never win a case by simply opening a textbook and reciting the law. We must always be able to explain how the law intersects with the *unique* facts of this case to create the outcome that our client seeks and how the law and the facts *link*. And as laws are constantly evolving, and facts are different every time, we must argue for a different linkage in every case.

This means that for each and every case, we must *create* a bespoke argument. Nothing can be taken from the shelf. So whether we like it or not, the element of creating remains present and cannot be escaped from.

Creative time

So creativity is essential. The next question is: how? How do we cultivate more creativity in our work?

If it exists, we must first dispense with the idea that *"I am not a creative person"*. Every one of us is equally capable of using both the left and right sides of our brains as the situation requires. A career focused on the strict logic of the situation may have left the required neurons slightly unused but nothing more. We are all equally capable of generating creativity, just as anyone can learn to tango, change a tyre or learn Japanese. Sulkily lurking around the edge of the dance floor, alleging an incapacity to "get down" will not fly. We can all do it: just get out there.

A far more legitimate barrier is finding the necessary time. Creativity can only flourish if allowed time and space to breathe. And while this sounds simple, for busy, in-demand and on-the-go lawyers, it can be incredibly hard. We are often waylaid and distracted by many more pressing tasks and engagements, which, like gases in a container, end up occupying all our available mental space.

It's easy to be sympathetic to this reality – we've all lived it and know it to be a frustrating truth. But we must nevertheless not give up on carving out time to think. We cannot live the entirety of our waking lives beholden to tasks, deadlines, and ticking the boxes. We must get space to think. As shown below, it's always possible.

Despite running one of the largest companies in the world, Bill Gates would take time out once a year and drive to a secluded log cabin for a "*Think Weekend*", consisting of nothing more than himself, copious amounts of soft drinks ("brain fuel") and a pile of papers for him to read and digest.

It was on one of these weekends in 1995 that he wrote a paper entitled "The Internet Tidal Wave",[8] predicting the explosion of the internet as a ubiquitous force that would change the world. Reading the memo now, his predictions are chillingly prescient:

- *"Amazingly, it is easier to find information on the Web than it is to find information on the Microsoft Corporate Network."*
- *"Customers will come to our 'home page' in unbelievable numbers and find out everything we want them to know."*

---

8 Gates, Bill. "The Internet Tidal Wave." Memo, 26 May 1995. https://www.justice.gov/sites/default/files/atr/legacy/2006/03/03/20.pdf.

- *"I believe the Internet will become our most important promotional vehicle, and paying people to include links to our home pages will be a worthwhile way to spend advertising dollars".*

Such (accurate) predictions reached on the weekend in the woods would ensure Microsoft capitalised early on the internet's rise ("*get involved and take advantage*", as Gates put it). This insight was worth billions to Microsoft shareholders and probably ensured, as it turns out, the continued existence of the enterprise.

The counterfactual is interesting to hypothesise: what if Gates had skipped that particular weekend, snowed under with urgent work, with the result Microsoft had missed the shifting technological sands and the nascent emergence of the internet, doubling down on "offline" technologies and ultimately went the way of Kodak?

How many great ideas will you never have because you are too manic to sit quietly and have them?

Of course, this didn't happen, and on balance, the world is probably better for it. But Microsoft (and us) were only saved because Gates prioritised taking time to *think*, to get away. To allow his mind to roam, digest and synthesise. The easy route would have been to stay in Seattle, working furiously long hours as CEO in his young company, just as the busier route calls us strongly as well.

But it's a trap: how many great ideas will you never have because you are too manic to sit quietly and have them?

Even the busiest lawyer could hardly claim to be busier than Gates in 1995. His maturity to recognise the need to step away to think is a commendable example to follow. If he can, we can.

The problem of "staying busy"

Another more subtle but nevertheless troublesome barrier to spending more time "*quietly thinking*" lies in how it intersects with the billable model.

Quiet thinking can either yield flashes of brilliance in a very short space of time or (more frequently, of course) nothing of value for hours of quiet reflection. In either case, the billable model is a poor fit. It simultaneously under-compensates the momentary brilliance while overcompensating the lawyer for sitting and doing several hours of nothing.

In addition to being a nice academic point, it is also painfully practical. Simply put, many clients will not like to see "*Thinking: 6 hours*" appear on the bill. While they may accept "*Drafting necessary court documents: 6 hours*" because there is a tangible activity and a tangibly useful product at the end, time charged for "*thinking*" can often (inaccurately) just seem like a con. What do you need to think about? Aren't you the expert? Don't you already know the answers?

This, of course, is a bit of a libel and unfair. If we want great arguments, we must apply creativity, and creativity can only flourish if mental space is allowed to germinate. But equitable or not, it's likely to be a real and common client objection that can further dissuade us from setting aside time for thinking. It feels far safer and less likely to antagonise the payer of the bills and to stay busy doing things than to slow down to think about things.

And the issue isn't just clients: we must also overcome our own prejudices. Imagine you were walking around the office and saw a colleague sitting, feet on the desk, looking out the window, for an hour. Be honest: what wouldn't your reaction be? What are they *doing*? Slacking off? Not working hard clearly. This is an internal peer pressure of which we are all aware. So we often make a conscious effort to be (or at least look) busy so as not to earn the disapprobation of our colleagues.

But we have to get out of the factory mindset, where if we are not constantly in frantic motion, we are not producing anything of value.

As an observation (not a brag), I once had an idea in a case that doubled the amount of money our client could claim, an argument that had hitherto been overlooked. Was I busting a gut typing for the entire day? Was I furiously researching? Was it pouring over the relevant legislation? Hardly. I was at my desk eating lunch. Yet this idea was worth hundreds of millions of dollars to our client. I worked on that case for eighteen months, yet those few seconds were more valuable than the rest of the time I spent on it combined.

The normal story of case preparation is slow and methodical, as you gradually value the case and put it through the conveyancing steps to try and monetise it. The rate of progress is slow and constant.

And then: bang! Eating lunch, the idea hits me. That single flash of brilliance doubled the value of the case (by doubling the amount of money claimable) despite taking almost no time at all. That's a very valuable sandwich. To take the structure introduced in the previous chapter, I inadvertently "improved" the case over lunch.

And it wasn't necessarily because I am brilliant. There is no innate genius in me that doesn't also reside in each and every one of us. It's just that by taking a quiet moment to myself and allowing my head to clear and wander, my mind was able (entirely without my conscious effort) to make a connection that I would never have seen if I had been deliberately looking for it. Eighteen months of hard work was outdone, instantly and exponentially, by a single moment of quiet inspiration.

And a colleague walking past would have thought, "*there's Sam, not working, taking a break*". How misleading.

And a colleague walking past would have thought, "there's Sam, not working, taking a break". How misleading.

We've all had similar experiences. The quiet, still moments often produce the ideas of the greatest weight. We must respect that silent, spiritual moment in ourselves and others when they have it. Never mistake the inactivity of others as evidence of their indolence.

As a quote I once heard says: *"As a manager, if I see someone staring hard out the window, I go over and congratulate them. I say "thank you for thinking".* Thought determines action, and actions determine results. If we want to be more effective litigators, we must follow the same example.

Improving creative thinking with techniques

If we have accepted the importance of creativity and set aside specific time (log cabin or otherwise) to think, what comes next?

Unfortunately, we can't demand that good ideas appear. However, we can improve the chances that they will stop by with the following techniques.

Brainstorming

The first technique is brainstorming. You can do this alone. If you do it with others, there are some rules.

First, lawyers love to attack ideas. To identify why something might not work. Of course, this helps test the idea and ensure it is sound by putting it through the wringer of scrutiny. But when *any* objection can scupper an idea (as it too often does in law), it promotes doing nothing. It's far more appropriate to test the idea, acknowledge the objection, and then ask, 'can we nevertheless overcome it?'

Any lawyer can find a reason why an argument won't work. Great lawyers find a way to make it work anyway.[9]

Any lawyer can find a reason why an argument won't work.
Great lawyers find a way to make it work anyway.

Rule two. Beware dominant personalities. Good ideas are statistically

9 This is not originally my quote. I picked this up from somewhere, but have no idea where.

distributed equally between quiet and loud people. Everyone must receive a fair audience.[10]

The third rule: start early. Legal positions solidify like concrete. The longer you leave it, the harder to change. It is rarely helpful to have a blinding insight on the eve of the trial.

Relocate

The second technique is to mix it up.

History tells us (Archimedes' Bath, Newton's Apple, Darwin's Finches) that the very best insights usually occur *away* from the desk. Undoubtedly, the foundation for these insights comes from deep study and hard work. Still, the additional 'spark' is often not combusted until the mind is relaxed doing something else.

We've all had the same experience. After studying a problem intensively, we were across the facts, but pushing harder for *insight* was futile. In frustration, we did something else. Running. Yoga. Listening to music. Then, 'ah hah!'

It happens surprisingly often. So do more of this. Replicate the pattern. Study hard, then mix it up. And who knows? Maybe one day everyone will know '[*Your Name*]'s Swimming Pool'.

Embrace the paradox that you get your best ideas for work while not working.

The importance of time management

The third technique for great ideas is good time management.

Admittedly, this does seem counter-intuitive. Isn't the concept of a carefully cultivated list of organised, regimented and ordered tasks the antithesis of creativity? Doesn't the crushing structure choke spontaneity?

But I don't find so. In my experience, being well organised doesn't just assist in being creative. It is actually – going one step further – an indispensable

10 Cain, Susan. Quiet: The Power of Introverts in a World That Can't Stop Talking. 2013.

prerequisite of creativity. When you are an excellent time manager, it actually unleashes your inner power.

You can use your head to think, not frantically keep track of tasks. The swirling eddy of ill-digested thoughts, loose ends, plans, dreams and hopes is a gnarly garden from which to propagate the seeds of a grand idea. It's dirty, messy and cluttered. Nothing can spring to life there.

The swirling eddy of ill-digested thoughts, loose ends, plans, dreams and hopes is a gnarly garden from which to propagate the seeds of a grand idea. It's dirty, messy and cluttered. Nothing can spring to life there.

The solution is to clean up your mind and implement a time and task management system that frees you from the crushing and choking "mental load" of tracking and managing deliverables in your head.

There are two ways to do it: do or delegate. In respect of the latter, some people delegate the "time management" aspect of their professional career entirely, becoming a sort of disorganised, eccentric creative genius who regularly has flashes of brilliance but barely answers an email and relies on others to manage the effort, monitor deadlines and deliverables, and even arrange for the gardening at their house. They are intellectual giants but children in every other respect. Others are more balanced, finding a way to "do" time management, recognising the need for both: basics first, then brilliance. They see getting organised as a preparatory exercise for brilliance, where the quiet relief and relaxation from knowing everything is accounted for frees their mind to roam. If I have to recommend a course, I commend the latter. In my view, such organised people are mature, well-rounded, very adult, and inevitably the best lawyers.

...a sort of disorganised, eccentric creative genius who regularly has flashes of brilliance but barely answers an email...

The Culling Step

Taking stock, where are we? By now, we have:

- accepted the need for creativity;
- carved out time to think and
- followed the above techniques (brainstorming, quiet thinking and good time management).

Hopefully, this means you have generated, as the fruits of your creative labour, a long list of potential arguments to deploy on behalf of your client in court. Fantastic job.

But now comes the really difficult bit – culling. Unfortunately, in any list of potential arguments we generate, particularly a long one, there will *inevitably* be some weak ones. Instances where creativity has misfired, where the dismissive euphemism "*it's very creative*" is appropriate. We must remove these arguments from further consideration.

This can be a little bruising to the ego, as our arguments are our intellectual children – the fruits of our professional creativity. But we must show no quarter. As Stephen King advises all authors in the editing stage: "*Kill your darlings*".

Because the danger of not culling weak arguments is clear. This classic example from Irving Younger shows just how foolish you can look if you indiscriminately throw every possible argument at the case:

"The plaintiff, a farmer who grew a patch of cabbages behind his house, had a neighbour who kept a goat in his backyard. One day, the goat broke loose, got into the cabbage patch and ate lots of cabbages while digging up and ruining the rest of the patch. The farmer sued the owner of the goat for his lost cabbages.

Here is how the 'raise-every-issue defence lawyer' responded in his opening statement:

" '*You had no cabbages.*

" '*If you had any cabbages, they were not eaten.*

" '*If your cabbages were eaten, it was not by a goat.*

" '*If a goat ate your cabbages, it wasn't my goat.*

" '*And if it was my goat, he was insane.*' "

The lesson we can derive is simple: at the bottom of any list of creatively produced arguments will lie one or two "*insane goats*". Don't run with these. "*Kill these darlings*", and move on.

Aside from eliminating the prospect of suppressed laughter, it's beneficial in other ways to keep your arguments short. A long list of arguments can simply betray a lack of confidence in any single one.

Practice, practice, practice

This leaves you with a short, strong list of ideas. Well done. But our work is still unfinished. The final step is to practice them.

Just as you wouldn't expect to kick your first ball at the World Cup final, similarly, we shouldn't expect arguments to debut successfully at trial for the very first time. It is essential to practice. Courts will not accept first drafts of written arguments. Why should they accept first drafts of oral ones?[11]

Without practice, we ask for trouble. Too frequently, arguments considered

11 With thanks to my colleague Ben Richards of Aticus.

strong on paper, or when rehearsed in our heads alone, collapse when subjected to the scrutiny of actual combat. The judge says, "*I don't get it*". Or "*I don't agree – what else have you got*"?

Human nature is partially to blame. We can very easily fall in love with our own cleverness when we spend much time in isolation, thinking about an argument. Familiarity inflates our expectations. We detach from reality.

But bitter experience tells me judges have no such rose-coloured glasses nor any hesitation calling out an emperor not wearing clothes. The gaps your ego skates over are often painfully obvious to more objective minds.

But bitter experience tells me judges have no such rose-coloured glasses nor any hesitation calling out an emperor not wearing clothes.

Practice, therefore, provides an important reality check. By asking uninvolved colleagues to sit as judge and opponent in a mock trial, we put our arguments through the crucible of actual combat. When forced to argue our position under fire to *convince* an impartial judge, the unconvincing arguments stand out. Surprisingly quickly.

Practice also serves another purpose. For the arguments that survive we can improve them. We can ask the judge what they liked, what they rejected, and what they might have accepted *if* it had just been a shade different. This is invaluable, especially if repeated with different judges, and can be used to refine our position further. Through multiple cycles, our arguments become clearer, more concise and more convincing. Just like in other industries, iterative improvements based on repeated feedback is the key to quality.

Without feedback, we are just guessing that our argument is persuasive. Logic is universal and can be assessed in the abstract. But persuasion is always in the eye of the beholder. Without testing our argument against a real-life opinion, we run into trial blind as to whether our points are actually likely to strike home.

To be clear: this is not rehearsing witness testimony, which in some jurisdictions is frowned upon. That is the witness practising what to say. This is the *lawyer* practising what to say: entirely different, completely appropriate, and utterly essential.

That is the witness practising what to say. This is the lawyer practising what to say.

The Rocket Launch

There is another reason to practice – to pass it up would be a slap in the face to the opportunity. There are many other instances of high-stakes work where people would kill for the opportunity for a dry run.

One such example is contemporary. As he was conceiving the ambitious Space X programme to colonise Mars, Elon Musk and his team ultimately had to figure out how to launch a rocket safely. As Mr Musk explained, this was incredibly difficult because the first practice was also the final exam. There is no opportunity to trial the rocket launch in advance – the only test is on launch day. Compounding the difficulty, this final exam has a 100% pass rate. When launching a rocket, anything but perfection is a failure.

This inability to rehearse is a challenging restraint. It compounds the difficulty of what is, literally, an exercise in rocket science.

But if that's accepted, why then when we have the opportunity to practice, refine and improve our arguments before trial, do we decline that same opportunity?

We regularly do so, but this strikes me as a folly. While there is no scope for a rocket to be truly tested in launch conditions other than the actual launch, the same is not true of legal arguments. They *can* be tested, practised, refined, the bugs streamlined, the loose threads trimmed, in a safe, secure and private space. With that in mind, it seems nonsensical to opt for the alternative: nervously sitting in mission control, hoping and praying that the unpractised arguments take flight in front of the judge at trial.

The brilliance of hindsight

Further, by practising several times, we also draw upon the powerful benefit of hindsight. The common lament of the litigator goes as follows:

In every case, I make three arguments. There is the argument I practice in my head before the hearing – logical, well-structured and clear. Next is the argument I actually present in court – disjointed, interrupted and stilted. Finally, there is the argument I think of when driving home – perfect, persuasive and devastating.

Finally, there is the argument I think of when driving home – perfect, persuasive and devastating.

Suppose we only present our argument once, at the actual trial. In that case, we generally have to be content with the disjointed argument representing the pinnacle of our case and have no opportunity to deploy the devastating argument we concocted in the car. Conversely, by practising several times, we get to deploy the wisdom of hindsight again and again until we have perfected the point – ready for the big day.

Costs

As an objection to practising, you might say: "*Isn't this practising business really expensive?*". And it is. But it is an investment, and as with any investment, we shouldn't judge the top-line costs, but only the bottom-line return. Practising is a *very* high return activity.

Let's assume our client is claiming $1 million in a lawsuit, and we judge they have a 50% chance of winning. Before practice, the case is, therefore, worth $500,000.

Let's also assume we hire three expensive people for two days. They read the background material, listened to live arguments several times, and gave feedback on what was persuasive and what was not. This costs $10,000.

To recoup our $10,000 investment, we only need a 1% increase in the chance of winning. (Increasing the case value to $510,000, or a $10,000 increase).

With the benefit of practice in a *live* situation against a real opponent and impartial judges, receiving feedback on your efforts achieving *at least* a 1% increase in the odds of winning should be easy, if not guaranteed.

Yes, this is an 'on paper' return. But so are home improvements, and that doesn't stop us from plundering hardware stores on the weekend.

So when seen in this light, while practising is expensive, it is hard to conceive a more effective use of our time. If expense remains a concern, consider what other less important activities could be done more economically or completely discontinued to free up the necessary resources.

Conclusion

Creativity is often used as a counterpoint to knowledge. Artists are creative, whereas good lawyers are deeply logical and fixed. This chapter has attempted to rescue the reputation of creativity and make an important point about its fundamental necessity.

In doing so, I did not intend to dismiss the value of other important legal skills. Logic is always necessary to support even the most creative argument. Scepticism must ensure your opponent's arguments are properly, robustly tested and challenged. An encyclopaedic recall of the law provides an advantage by equipping you with the ability to generate more ideas. To see more possible connections, generate new insights, and inspire different possible angles of attack.

But such knowledge is the starting point, not the end. Turning these intangible ideas into concrete arguments will always still require *creativity*, not a simple rote application. In preparing the best arguments, we must start with the rigour of logic, knowledge and alike, but ultimately sprinkle it with the dust of *imagination*. The relationship between logic and creativity is, in this way, linearly symbiotic.

It is said that a strong head and a strong heart are a powerful combination. Lawyers tend to have no problem providing the head when making arguments. I say we should, through the prism of creativity, learn to embrace a liberal dose of heart as well.

As I said above, the entire point of preparing for trial is to arrive at trial with something compelling to say. We shouldn't waste this opportunity with staid recitations of fact and law – we must get creative.

The entire point of preparing for trial is to arrive at trial with something compelling to say.

CHAPTER 6 - SETTLING

"Discourage litigation. Persuade your neighbors to compromise whenever you can. Point out to them how the nominal winner is often a real loser — in fees, expenses, and waste of time. As a peacemaker the lawyer has a superior opportunity of being a good man. There will still be business enough."

- Abraham Lincoln

Settling a case is like buying a car. It's a transaction. So, cases only settle if the parties:

1. agree on what the case is worth, and
2. want to do a deal.

If we want to improve settlement rates (as Mr Lincoln beseeched), we must nurture these pre-conditions.

Agreement

To agree on what the case is worth, each side must value it. This requires three Ms:

- Method
- Materials
- Mindset

Method

We must first consider technique. How is litigation valued?

Common cases are valued like antiques – experience and gut feel. The personal injury lawyer says, *"whiplash is worth $150,000 on a good day"*. The lawyer is not making a calculation. They are leaning on the wisdom of history.

Over time, a *"going settlement rate"* emerges for particular types of cases, which lawyers can adjust up (or down) depending on the circumstances of their particular case. This makes valuing common cases relatively straightforward.

But *uncommon* or *unique* cases, by definition, cannot be valued from experience. Valuation requires mathematics: the lawyer's assessment of the chance of winning (%) is usually multiplied by the amount claimed ($).

"You claim $100,000, and I judge you have a 50% chance of winning. Therefore, your case is worth $50,000."

While this is not an exact science, it works well in simple cases. It is in large, complex cases that we hit problems.

In complex cases, uncovering *what happened* takes time. Until the facts settle, lawyers may feel uncomfortable assessing the likelihood (%) of winning. The window to settle comes late.

Even when the moment arises, the formula struggles with complexity. My case has seven different arguments of varying strengths, some depending on what witnesses will say, and each of which will earn a different recovery – how do I put it all in the formula?

But most fatally, even if you tame the formula, what if you miscalculate? Even a 1% mistake in a large case is an expensive professional error. Lawyers are, therefore, hesitant to recommend large settlement amounts.

So, it is rare to settle big, unique cases. Lawyers perceive valuations as too hard and too risky. But if you can't settle, you must win. And the resulting arms race is expensive.

But if you can't settle, you must win. And the resulting arms race is expensive.

What would work?

Training. Inescapably, lawyers must be better, more confident *valuers* of litigation. Methodologies exist[12]. Unfortunately, it is one of those numerous skills which, while very important in practice, is often conspicuously absent from the law school curriculum.

Safety nets also help, so insurers must offer cover for large valuation mistakes. Increased premiums (passed onto clients) will be offset by savings (made by clients) when cases settle earlier.

Material

Once we know how to value the case (or any asset), we need the *information* to do it. "*How many miles has it done?*" "*How many bedrooms does it have?*"

For litigation, the relevant information is as follows:

- the facts (what happened), and
- the law (the consequences).

Assuming competent advice, information about the law is equally available. But facts are not. Except for the simplest cases, knowledge is asymmetrically distributed. Each side only knows (at most) what their witnesses and documents

---

12 See John Celona, Winning at Litigation through Decision Analysis: Creating and Executing Winning Strategies in any Litigation or Dispute (Springer, 2016).

know (and how convincing they are). The other side remains hidden.

This hinders settlement. After all, you can't value a house without seeing half the rooms!

You can't value a house without seeing half the rooms.

My first case was a good illustration of the problem. I was defending a truck company. A driver allegedly struck a pothole at the depot and jarred his back. Perplexingly, an inspection of the depot showed no potholes (I know, I went out there).

We met to attempt a settlement. The driver's eminent lawyer railed at length about his client's poor back. Undoubtedly true, but where was the pothole? Plucking my courage, I ventured:

"Ah, thanks, James. I can see that your client's injury is significant. I think the real issue we're having from our perspective…it's a little unclear exactly what the precise mechanism of the injury was…would your client be willing to clarify exactly where this, ah, hole was in relation to the …?"

James' interjection was swift:

"We're not disclosing that! What do you think we are, complete idiots?"

Bludgeoned into silence, I shut up. James switched targets, no beat skipped, next decrying our "*lax maintenance*". When the monologue concluded, I left.

James's response is typical of litigation – disclose little and get angry. Was I intimidated? I sure was! But was I *convinced*?

No. Like advertising, James had presented an incomplete and exaggerated version of the truth. He withheld key information. This left me with no reliable data to value the case (how did I know if the hole was a tiny crack or gaping crater), and it didn't settle. How could it?

What would work

Honesty. Coyness and partial disclosure are common in litigation. But as valuation requires complete information, this frustrates settlement.

To sell the house, you must allow a full inspection. Candour is mandatory. You must disclose all you know. And be entitled to the same in return.

This *can* be pushed too far. We must not trample the needs of confidentiality and privilege. And disclosing *everything* can be expensive. But equally, we must not be held hostage to these ideas – the more information we suppress, the less likely the case is to settle.

Mindset

So we know *how* to value and know we must be candid with our opponents. But that's not enough. Accurate valuation also requires candour with ourselves.

This is harder than it sounds. Advocates often get overconfident in litigation. In our utmost effort to craft winning arguments, we can be trapped into believing in the total merit of the case, in our divine favour, and that our arguments must inevitably prevail. But this is not the mindset to value accurately. If we are passionately in love with our car, house, or case will probably overvalue it.

Being fair, our approach is partially defensible. A common prerequisite for compelling advocacy is *belief*. Absent believing in your client's cause, being hired is unlikely, and a lacklustre presentation to the decision-maker is assured. Clients want, and society expects, us to be *fierce* advocates, not academically dry ones.

But we must not get carried away. We must not be seduced by our own cleverness. We must have the professional integrity to stand back and think from time to time. How strong is our case – *really*? The ideal litigator can change speed between fierce advocacy and quiet reflection (or, as in Chapter 1, get someone else to). Only then can we (or they) fairly value the case.

The alternative is each lawyer, in their passion, overestimates the chance of victory. Only at the door of the court, or after the case starts and the fantasy unravels, does reality strike. "*The case is not as strong as we thought. We are vulnerable. We have to settle!*" But the light should have dawned earlier.

What would work instead?

Objectivity. While some belief is necessary for good advocacy, and confidence is reassuring for the client, the client is not otherwise served by unsupportable proclamations of surety. If both generals are equally optimistic, there will be no peace.

The client is not served by unsupportable proclamations of surety.

We must balance reassuring optimism with clear-eyed realism. Only then can we accurately value the case and have the right mindset to settle.

Upset clients

An accurate valuation is the first step. But there is a second. The client must *want* to settle.

This is also a common hurdle. Litigation can make people emotional. Upset. Angry even. And in this state, rather than recognising all litigation has a price, it becomes a crusade, where anything less than total victory is unacceptable capitulation. For this reason, embroiled clients often resist settlement efforts (even good deals). Emotion clouds judgement.

Also, sometimes, it's not about the money. A client's motivation may not be primarily economic. *It's for the principle. We want to create a new law. I've come too far to settle now.* Such mindsets may be noble but are a menace to settlement efforts. How does offering cash entice you to quit if it's not about the money?

What would work instead?

Anger management. It is good advice to count to ten before losing your temper. It is similarly prudent for clients not to make settlement decisions when upset.

Lawyers have an important, almost paternal, role to play here. We must help the client see litigation through a dispassionate lens. A lens where dollars and sense drive decisions, not hurt feelings.

Personal injury litigation provides a good example of neutralising unhelpful emotion. The *"no win, no fee"* arrangement takes the settlement decision from the (emotional) client. It bestows it paternalistically on the (unemotional) lawyer. Settlement rates in these disputes are very high.[13]

Conversely, in family law matters, clients are often *very* upset but retain their hands on the wheel of the settlement decision – settlement is far rarer. Emotion clouds the sensible way.

Conclusion

Whether a car or a company, transactions generate net wealth for society. Deals are a *good thing*. Settlement is no different.

But we do not achieve deals by simply imploring litigants and lawyers to "*try and settle*". Nor should cases be settled out of fear, fatigue or finger-in-the-air assessments of case value. No less than other areas of the economy, a properly functioning settlement market requires scientific valuations, plenty of information and a cool head – not coercion or exhaustion.

No less than other areas of the economy, a properly functioning settlement market requires scientific valuations, plenty of information and a cool head – not coercion or exhaustion.

Of course, we may not want the case to settle. Or we may think the new skills, cultural shift and increased candour are too high a price to pay for

13 Noting also that in no win no fee, lawyers often are incentivised to settle early and claim the "fee" that comes from the "win" (the settlement counting as a win). Plus, with little information asymmetry and lots of accumulated cases to give a going settlement rate, settlement conditions are very favourable.

increasing settlement rates. This is a legitimate perspective.

But we cannot have our cake and eat it too. If we want more cases to settle and live up to Mr Lincoln's timeless mandate, this is the unavoidable cost.

PART 2
HOW MUCH

CHAPTER 7 - WHY SELL?

"Nothing happens until a sale is made"

- Thomas J Watson (1874 – 1956)

To sell something, you have to overcome objections and explain the benefits. To sell lawyers on the '*idea of selling*', the same structure works.

Overcoming objections

Let's start with objections. There are three main ones:

1. Marketing is unnecessary;
2. If it's necessary, it's not my job;
3. If it's my job, I don't like doing it.

It's unnecessary

The first objection: it's unnecessary because the best marketing is doing good work. Doing good work brings more work.

True. But only from the same clients. Other clients will always be reluctant to switch. Why should they? Their incumbent has the considerable advantage of being a known quantity. While you might be better, you might be worse. This can be an unacceptable risk.

It is just so much easier and less of a gamble for the client to stick with an existing provider.

Hence, the flow of litigation work is stable. You'll get more from current clients and little from others by doing good work. This can be temptingly comfortable. But it's also a time bomb. As few clients need a litigator forever, eventually, work will stop.

The only defence is proactivity. We must get out and shake the tree. Pitch to new people while we can and before we must. Sell ourselves so convincingly that a new client overcomes inertia and is forced by intellectual honesty to try something new. You.

So, doing good work? Not enough. You have to tell others about it. And get them to hire you, too. That's marketing. The bare minimum required for a long and varied career.

Someone else's job

The second objection is: where is the firm? Surely, it's their responsibility to win the work. We'll focus on doing it.

But no, again. We cannot abrogate responsibility. Our value exists in non-transferable and nebulous *"experience and judgement"*. Only we can convey its value. Not a marketing executive.

History, in any case, has largely invalidated the logic of coordinating production centrally rather than relying on individual entrepreneurialism. This makes sense. It is easier to be nimble individually than expect a behemoth firm to change course to capitalise on every opportunity.

I don't like it

Third objection: we begrudgingly acknowledge that marketing is necessary and our responsibility. But we don't like it.

Self-promotion

Many worry that marketing will require excessive self-promotion. A sort of icky narcissism. We, of course, worry this will be off-putting. Humans love speaking about themselves but (somewhat hypocritically, I suppose) find it tiresome when others do so excessively.

But this suggests a solution. We do not need to fear excessive self-promotion, as it is ineffective anyway. It is better to redirect the marketing conversation so your client can talk about their favourite topic: themselves.[14]

We often don't have enough focus on the recipient of the work. Instead, marketing seems to become an effort to prove how great you are. This is fine – but it must be balanced with a focus on the client, what makes them great, and what leaves them in need of your help.

So seen, marketing done properly shouldn't require excessive and uncomfortable self-inflation.

Difficulty

We are also concerned that marketing is hard. Undoubtedly. But since was this an excuse?

Many medicines are unappetising, and many things that are good for us are difficult. We do (or should do) them anyway.

We should challenge our thinking further, too. How hard *should* it be? Many of us are trained advocates. We are home in the cut and thrust of arguments, objections, points, and counterpoints. We are paid to be persuasive in the face of opposition.

Should we not also feel a natural comfort with being similarly compelling in our attempts to convince clients to engage our services? Could it not be said – if we can't convince the potential client now, how will we manage to convince the decision maker ultimately? Harsh conclusion or trenchant insight? I leave it to the reader to ponder.

---

14 Dale Carnegie, How to Win Friends and Influence People (Simon & Schuster, 2009).

Benefits

Having dealt with the objections, it's time for the benefits. Most obviously, selling is important for fiscal success. You don't have a career if you have a skill but no customers. You have a hobby.

But even if the money holds no sway over you, other compelling benefits exist.

Utilitarianism

Utilitarian perspective first. You are an asset. And the market abhors a disused asset or an asset not in its highest and best use. The opportunity cost harms the owner and deprives society of a fully productive, value-contributing unit. So selling helps society. Our asset pulls its weight.

Personal

Personal perspective next. No one wants to be useless. But without selling, our skills and judgement, crafted (to take the panoramic view) across an entire educational and working lifetime, lie unused. Without use. Useless.

This is very wasteful. The expensive Ferrari does not wish to be confined to the garage. It wishes to attack the road, to be released into the environment for which it was created. It wants to be free.

It fears the alternative. It fears a dark garage. It fears sitting alone and depreciating, with only the echoes for company and the only roar coming from the increasingly deafening melancholy as the outside world forgets.

Is this our fate? If we fail to market, it will be. We will have no work to do. The garage will remain shut.

Marketing is, therefore, a rallying cry. It is incumbent on us not to allow our skills to lie decrepit. To not waste our chance, to strive for a sale that fully employs our unique talents, and to recapture our place on the road.

Because life is short, very short. A mere blink to the world that will continue on happily without us. We mustn't waste in the garage.

Evolutionary

Evolutionary perspective, finally. Successful marketing is a proxy for demonstrating value. We all claim to be the best, but the only true test of excellence is whether your clients trade valuable resources to engage your services. The iron law of the market says it cannot be otherwise.

But there is an elegance to this economic Darwinism. Forcing each of us to market forces us to remain relevant to the market's needs. An ever-evolving market. Selling should, therefore be welcomed as the compelling force which keeps us fresh and modern, in countenance to the weight of tradition, which often pulls in the other direction.

If we don't want to serve the market and study law for its own sake only, an academic career will suit us better.

Our careers

Speaking of careers, marketing benefits this too.

Unstructured career

The great excitement (and challenge) of law is that the path of progress is not prescriptive or linear.

Whereas professions such as medicine have tightly controlled career options (general practice, different variations of surgery, etc.), in law, there is no overarching structure to work towards. Nor to fit into.

Do you want to be a disputes lawyer specialising in outback pastoral leases? Why not. Do you want to be a personal injury lawyer specialising in assisting teachers who have burnt out through overwork? Go for it. Do you want to limit yourself to defending shareholder class actions against pharmaceutical companies for failure to update the market of a material change in the research prospects of a new product? You bet. The available permutations are as diverse as your imagination.

Even better, should you decide after several years that you know all there is to know about (say) patent litigation and would like to try criminal law – the answer (at least from an architectural perspective of the profession) is a resounding "*why not*"? The ability to work in a niche you find thrilling and fascinating, switching as you please, is a great opportunity for the law.

The opportunity has another dimension as well. As opposed to medicine, it is as legitimate to specialise in a particular type of client (patient) as in a particular law area. While the clients in medicine are – within a few standard deviations – all homo sapiens, there is a far more diverse legal ecosystem to explore. Want to only act for FTSE500 companies? Individual rock stars? Sporting clubs? You can! It's a blank canvas.

But total freedom brings two challenges.

First, it is unstructured, and no one will tell you what to do. You have to decide for yourself. For many lawyers swept along in the "did well at school, wasn't sure what to study, so did law, finished it and thought might as well practice, pass the bar and look up and go – how did I get here?", this is a decision point we can be guilty of neglecting. Faced with a blank canvas, we get writer's block.

The second challenge is that you can only work in your chosen speciality if you can convince people to hire you in this area. Thus, the importance of selling. You can't be the world's pre-eminent construction arbitration specialist if you can't convince anyone to hire you to do this. Successful selling is inevitably a prerequisite to fully exploring the law's blank canvas.

Conclusion

This chapter tried to sell selling. You've been given the arguments and heard the pitch.

Your question is: do you buy it? And can you afford not to?

The most frequent threat we face to our careers is our unwillingness to sell. Almost inevitably, when we feel periods of stagnation, it is because we have not been proactive enough in the past at marketing for the present.

The onus is on us. We may have work today, but we must secure tomorrow's work. Many lawyers object that they didn't *become* lawyers to sell. Still, the reality is that we cannot *remain* lawyers without it.

Without selling, we suffer what ancient fate heroes considered worse than death: obscurity.

However, we needn't begrudge it because marketing is an exciting opportunity to remain fresh, current and relevant. To expand our horizons and shape our careers. To work on things that make us happy, where we can make the maximum contribution, and where we can facilitate good in the world in what ultimately is a very brief life.

And that is why we sell.

CHAPTER 8 - REJECTION

"If you are holding out for universal popularity, I'm afraid you will be in this cabin for a very long time."

- J.K. Rowling

So why don't we do it? (Sell, that is). Excuses abound:

- I am too busy;
- I am too young;
- I am too old;
- No one will hire me;
- Selling is unprofessional;
- I don't know how;
- I don't want to seem pushy;
- Others are responsible for that;
- I don't want to offend a friend;
- I don't know anything about that area;
- I'm not a rainmaker.

Curiously, we let these excuses stop us. If the barrier to writing a piece of advice were a lack of knowledge, we would read, learn, and make it happen.

This suggests something else is going on, something not related to our capabilities but to our mindset. I posit that whatever the ostensible objection, our real barrier to marketing is our understandable *fear of rejection*.

A simple test proves it. How many people would you market to right now if you were guaranteed they would say yes? 10? 100? 1000? Suddenly, the excuses above don't seem so valid.

The fear

Lawyers hold no monopoly over the fear of rejection. It is universally hated. For instance, the popularity of dating apps can be explained (I am told) because they eliminate painful rejection. You express an interest. If unreciprocated, you can rationalise. "They must be away". Or "they rejected my profile, not me".

The ability to fool oneself, like a firing squad given a blank cartridge, attracts people to online dating. It provides a low-risk way to meet someone. A safety net preventing painful bruises to the ego.

But sadly, in selling, there are no guarantees. Rejection is inevitable. And no amount of talent or training can eliminate it.

Being fearless

On this analysis, while we can improve our marketing *skills* (a worthy task), the more important challenge is improving our marketing *attitude*. This requires that we embrace the inevitability of rejection.

Consider how different our marketing efforts would be if we were fearless.

We would try and sell our services with greater frequency. We would *ask* to be hired. Not skirt the issue by giving speeches or writing articles, hoping to attract work passively. By the law of averages, our sales would increase. Clients would probably describe us as '*proactive*', '*eager*', and '*hungry to help*' (even those that said no). Our efforts would eventually reach critical mass, as work often begets more work. Soon, we would be turning people away.

A litigator who had conquered the fear of rejection, even with only rudimentary marketing *skills*, would be a powerful rainmaker indeed.

A litigator who had conquered the fear of rejection, even with only rudimentary marketing skills, would be a powerful rainmaker indeed.

But conversely, without overcoming it, fear is a paralytic roadblock.

How do you conquer the fear?

The $64 question. It's not (intellectually) difficult. Similar to overcoming childhood fears – the three-metre diving board, crabs, falling off a bike – the trick is to do it once, see that nothing bad happens, and then go again. And again. Until the fear evaporates, the repeated exposure having hardened our resolve.

The problem is that many litigators never get sufficient rejections to develop this thick skin. We capitulate prematurely. This leaves us stranded on the wrong side of the fear curve.

Developing fearlessness

What can be done? There are several things a firm can do to help its lawyers.

Individual support

One solution, like with nervous children, is support. Dad helped us down the waterslide the first time. Even as adults, we still need encouragement to try new things. Fear is never outgrown, only redirected.

Who might support us?

- A lawyer. To be most credible, this person should empathise with your challenges – personally, having lived them, not just logically, because you have described them.
- A good marketer. It is disingenuous to ask you to do something they can't.
- Someone whom you want to impress. You will work harder to win their approval.
- Creative. Many sales opportunities (as many opportunities in life) occur serendipitously. This person must be able to help cultivate those chance connections and encounters.

Repetition destroys fear. And the missing ingredient to get started? Someone at the bottom of the slide.

Support in teams

Law firms can also create teams. Teams create accountability.

For this reason, paratroopers are put through their first jump as a squad. Peer pressure and the instructor's demands usually get even the most reluctant trainee out of the back of the plane.

It's a healthy dynamic to replicate. Not wanting to disappoint your colleagues is a powerful motivator to persist.

Measure the right things

What is measured is managed. As the primary challenge is getting lawyers to overcome their fears, their determination to do so should be tracked. So monitor *effort*.

In war, we celebrate those who return and those whom we lost in the pursuit of the cause, whose contribution is no less crucial to the overall effort.

In war, we celebrate those who return and those whom we lost in the pursuit of the cause, whose contribution is no less crucial to the overall effort.

In marketing, rejections (like casualties) are the unpleasant but inevitable cost of marketing success. Lawyers ploughing through rejections are trailblazers and warrant equal recognition. So monitor and encourage *effort*, and the results, through the weight of numbers, will take care of themselves.

Financial investment

It is expensive to do new things. There is a significant opportunity cost in being (initially) incompetent.

But this is another excellent point for the firm to step up. Suppose it wants to reap the benefits of excellent marketers tomorrow. In that case, it must support them in their tentative first steps today. All lawyers must be paid the same, regardless of their initial ineptitude.

This can be expensive. But remember, undisturbed salaries are not a gift. They are an investment. The firm can determine the vibrancy of its practice in twelve months by the degree to which it encourages and supports people to take up marketing today.

Our challenge

But we can't delegate everything to someone else. Individuals need to step up, too.

Letting go of perfection

Our coaches are tolerant of failure. We should be, too.

In our professional world, we avoid being *wrong* at all costs. Lawyers are perfectionists. Quality is paramount. While admirable in many ways, this environment does little to encourage us to branch out to unfamiliar things.

But we need to relax this attitude somewhat. Developing skills takes time. It can't be perfect immediately. Our first couple of marketing attempts will be clumsy. And that's ok. It's the price of experimenting. Missing a few shots won't kill you. In fact, few mistakes will.

Persistence

Many lawyers summon the courage to try marketing but stop immediately when it doesn't pay off.

The stopping is problematic. You don't get results from going to the gym once. A healthy body requires consistent, methodical attendance hundreds and hundreds of times.

You don't get results from going to the gym once.

To market successfully, you have to be in the long game. Lots of effort. Lots of rejection. You have to accept that nothing, least of all marketing success, can be achieved quickly.

Recalibrating perspective

Many lawyers' fears are based on a worst-case outcome. We are surrounded by calamity, which can colour our perception of how common it actually is. To lawyers, '*what's the worst that could happen*' is not a call to action. It's a legitimate question.

With marketing, our worst fear is being shamed, ridiculed, and scorned. Of course, this is *possible*. Some people are unkind. But it's also very unlikely.

Refusing to act because of the threat of the worst possible outcome (however remote) is not a logical basis for making decisions.

Refusing to act because of the threat of the worst possible outcome (however remote) is not a logical basis for making decisions.

For instance, there is a risk that a manned mission to Mars will encounter a previously unknown hostile lifeform, triggering an interstellar conflict that threatens the human race. It cannot be ruled out. But should far-fetched notions guide our actions?

Lawyers are apt to identify far-fetched eventualities, but the important dimension of probability is often absent[15]. A risk is only a problem if it is high impact *and* high risk. Many lawyers' predictions about what disaster could befall them if they try and market (*I will be forever known as an unprofessional hustler only interested in cash!*) fall into the realm of theoretical possibility (like most things) but of a such a tiny percentage of occurring that they are of practical irrelevance.

Conclusion

No marriage ever happened without someone asking: '*can I have your number*'. Selling is the same. You must endure the chance of rejection to get the rewards.

No marriage ever happened without someone asking: 'can I have your number'.

---

15 With thanks to my friend Nathan Zhivov.

This remains the most important marketing challenge for lawyers to overcome. We *can* obtain the necessary skills. But for most lawyers, the problem is not a lack of skills or a problem of style. It's a fear of asking.

The solution is to ask, ask, and ask again. Obviously, there is a right and a wrong way to do this. A balance between eagerness and impetuous. But we must ask. We must say, *"I think I can help. Will you hire me?"*

Without the courage to inquire, even the most strategically sound "*business development plan*", "*account maximisation methodology*", or "*marketing inroads roadmap*" can achieve nothing.

Improving our sales success is not primarily or even partially an intellectual challenge. We can all do it. The larger problem is how we, as real living, breathing (and mentally fragile) humans, can overcome our fears.

CHAPTER 9 - STATISTICS TELL THE STORY

"People ... operate with beliefs and biases. To the extent you can eliminate both and replace them with data, you gain a clear advantage."

- Michael Lewis

If you wanted to know whether someone was a good archer, you would ask, "*how many targets have you hit in your career?*".[16] You wouldn't care:

- how long they had been an archer;
- what club leadership positions they held;
- how well they knew all the terminology;
- whether they hit a target once and Hollywood made a film about it;
- how high their media profile is, or;
- how nice their uniform was.

16 Martire, Kristy A, and Gary Edmond. "Rethinking Expert Opinion Evidence." Melbourne University Law Review 40, no. 3 (2017).

You would want to know: *"how many targets have you hit?"*.

We do this because of the inescapable logic of statistics. While not infallible or impervious to manipulation, stats often provide the surest form of assessing any professional tasked with achieving results.

Who would judge a basketball player on anything other than points scored, a salesperson on anything but sales closed, or a chess grandmaster on games won?

How litigators are currently measured

But here's the curious thing. This is not normally done in law, despite the ability to measure lawyers objectively on the "percentage of cases" won.

Instead, judgements are made on a variety of things that are far less scientific, namely:

- The outcome of individual cases or;
- How the lawyer "looks", how high their media profile is, and how long they have been a lawyer or similar.

Of course, like our archer, these attributes are irrelevant when assessing competence. But they have been long-standing and pervasive.

Individual cases

Lawyers that win high-profile cases, especially if acting for a perceived "underdog", are often regarded, on that single piece of evidence alone, as being brilliant. Using these criteria of competence, lawyers who won famous cases such as Erin Brockovich, the 'Rainmaker' and Lt Caffey represent the apex of the profession. Their fame, and their fame alone, justifies the conclusion that they are fantastic.

And the inverse logic applies as well – lawyers who lose the big cases are forever tainted with the smear of incompetence (who remembers the lawyer Ms Brockovich prevailed over, for instance? They have gone down in history as just another in the litany of forgotten losers).

Now, of course, there is no reason why Erin Brockovich, the 'Rainmaker' and Lt Caffey could not be excellent litigators. They might be fantastic litigators. However, it is not particularly scientific to reach this conclusion based on *one* case alone.

This is because litigation is uncertain, dubious and chaotic. There are just too many things that happen in any one case that can cause it to be won (or lost) but are attributable to nothing more than the "luck" of the draw.

For instance:

- A smoking gun document is found;
- A key witness tells a new story on cross-examination;
- A sympathetic (or unsympathetic) judge is allocated;
- Parliament changes the law retrospectively;
- The defendant dramatically changes their story and admits, "*I did it*".

Given that victory in any *one* case may be attributable to good management *or* good luck, forming sweeping generalised conclusions about legal competence based on a single case outcome is not particularly scientific.

The look

The other traditional metric for assessing litigators is how they "look". Do they have the right suit, the right hair, the right media profile, the right background and the right firm?

This, of course, is in no way logically linked to the lawyer's capacity to achieve results, but in the absence of anything else, tends (in conjunction with individual results) to form the basis of a hiring decision.

This benefits those who, by luck and genetics, happen to look like what we expect a lawyer to look like, those who correlate most closely to the mental image of a lawyer we carry around in our minds. Of course, this heuristic is no foundation for sensible decisions, any more than a steam engine is the best type of train simply because that's what many people mentally conjure up when the word train is uttered.

Separating the best from the rest

But if we can't rely on single-case outcomes or the "look", how do we determine which litigators are truly the best?

To make an informed call, we should revert to the best evidence there is – statistical results. While the outcome of a *single* case might be attributable to luck, average litigation results over a large portfolio of cases *is* a much stronger indicator of performance.

It's much harder to dismiss regular, repeated results (whether good or bad) as being down to "chance". While you might get "*lucky*" once, is it fair to the lawyer who wins 50 cases in a row to accuse them of being on the blessed side of luck?

In fact, it would be the opposite. We would equate this long-term success as being strong demonstrative evidence of competence. Because while a talented lawyer applying their skill, ingenuity and effort to a case will still lose occasionally, *over the long run*, they will (by statistical force) have far more wins than losses.

And, equally, while the unskilled lawyer may get "*lucky*" on any one case, we would expect their lack of talent to catch up with them to produce far more losses than wins over the long run.

So while it is sometimes tempting, in the excitement of winning or bitterness of losing, to sing the praises of, or complain bitterly about, the competence of a lawyer, this is not logical. One case tells us very little. Indeed, if we judged the lawyer based on one case alone, we could easily reach the wrong conclusion

The better approach is to look at a wider range of results. We do not judge basketball players on whether they made one shot in isolation, and we shouldn't judge lawyers based on a single isolated result. Basketballers and lawyers should be judged on their long-term records. Only then does the chance they "*got lucky*" sufficiently diminish for us to make an informed decision about their talents.

Marketing

As an idea, a statistical-led approach represents a radical departure from historical marketing orthodoxy. But there is opportunity in it as well. Because long-term records are strong indicators of competence, statistics can be a powerful credibility enhancer to the lawyer with the right numbers.

Traditionally marketing of litigators relies on poetic descriptions over hard data. And while general phrases such as: "*has advised on [x,y and z] and delivers timely, practical and commercially focused advice*" may be true if withdrawn to a high enough level of abstraction, would you recruit a baseball player on such a description alone? Probably not. You'd want to see some data! Yet, this is what many clients have to be content with.

What is more helpful and frankly convincing is evidence of results. That's what the client buys when they buy you – the results you have achieved and can achieve as an advocate. So, mix some data with your poetry. If you are the truly excellent litigator you claim, divulge your track record and *prove* it. Statistically.

> *"Yes, we have acted in 20 cases like yours, and we achieved judgement in our favour in eight, while another ten were settled favourably. We analysed the two cases we lost and are very comfortable (and the clients were very comfortable) with our performance. In those cases, the client took a calculated gamble and lost. Still, we always knew (and had advised) that was a possibility. So, how can we help?"*

It can even be punchier than this. The pitch of one Chicago-based trial lawyer is illustrative. It says: "*In the last five years, he has tried 31 cases and won 28*"[17]. This testimonial, devoid of the normal marketing flourishes but impeccably clear, leaves us in no doubt. It is an unimpeachable, quantitative

17 NetworkTrialLawFirms, 'EVERYTHING ABOUT COUNSEL SELECTION THAT YOU WERE AFRAID TO ASK' (YouTube, accessed 6 October 2023) https://www.youtube.com/watch?v=PK2SMIOHYig.

record that speaks for itself, and it would, therefore, be unsurprising if he were one of America's most sought-after litigators.

So if you are good, say so. People with nothing to hide are content to rely on facts. Let others who need it rely on the obfuscation of marketing speak.

People with nothing to hide are content to rely on facts.

Asking directly

At this point, you may be reflecting on your own numbers. Do you feel squeamish?

That's quite common. The same trial lawyer observes, if asked point blank, *"how many cases have you won in the last five years?"*[18] many lawyers will probably express some mild surprise, then give one of two answers. A direct one. Or an evasive one couched in caveats: *"Well, you've got to understand ...."*[19]

The latter (for a client) is not a good sign. It reminds me of a story Dad told me when I was younger about installing a new front fence:

"I asked the builder how much it would cost. The builder winced slightly, sucked in some breath and said, "well, you've got to understand...."

Dad let the phrase hang in the air for a moment, then continued with a rueful smile:

"Sam, I've realised when someone starts answering with the phrase "well you have to understand...", you know you're not going to like the rest of it".

It's true. Answering what should be a mathematical question with qualifiers

---

18 NetworkTrialLawFirms, 'EVERYTHING ABOUT COUNSEL SELECTION THAT YOU WERE AFRAID TO ASK' (YouTube, accessed 6 October 2023) https://www.youtube.com/watch?v=PK2SMIOHYig.

19 NetworkTrialLawFirms, 'EVERYTHING ABOUT COUNSEL SELECTION THAT YOU WERE AFRAID TO ASK' (YouTube, accessed 6 October 2023) https://www.youtube.com/watch?v=PK2SMIOHYig.

and equivocation suggests that the underlying numbers are not flattering. So, if your first instinct is to qualify your answer, perhaps it's time to think about improving the underlying data (either at an individual or team level).

Objectivity

Of course, it's never just about us, and with statistics, it's no different. From a wider perspective, referencing statistics has another benefit: it provides an unequivocal, profession-wide guide to professional competence. This is something legal professionals (and many other professionals) sorely lack.

Clients at present are forced to revert to various imprecise and unscientific proxies to gauge comparative competence when comparing two lawyers. Single case outcomes. Age. The sharpness of dress. Educational institution attended. Familiarity. The law firm employed by. Years of experience. And especially, not previously mentioned, cost. The problem of cost. For when there are no objective measurements of quality, it is equal parts inevitable and unfortunate that a lawyer's hourly charge-out rate ($100 or $1000 per hour) becomes the misleading metric by which competence is assessed. The argument runs: the cost is higher. Therefore, the quality must be higher.

(We see the same thing with bottled water. Two bottles have the same water, with identical chemical make-ups and equivalent volumes. Yet the customer perceives Evian as "superior" to a generic brand purely on the logically irrelevant but psychologically persuasive basis of price.)

This tendency to measure lawyers on factors that have nothing to do with actual skill is problematic for at least two reasons.

First, clients run the significant risk of picking the wrong lawyer, having been led astray by a litany of red herrings (they were a big firm, cost heaps and just looked the part).

But the problem runs deeper. More widely, it leaves the industry impervious to new ways of performing litigation or new providers. For when there is no objective metric by which an expensive "traditional" law firm can be compared against an upstart firm, company or individual, the almost irresistible tendency is for clients to defer to the "safe" choice. The incumbent. The (unquantified) "reliable" pair of hands. This leaves litigation work overwhelmingly in the hands of a select few persons and firms who might "look the part" or to whom work has traditionally been trusted and prevents the diversification of the profession.

The sin of the status quo can be cleansed with data. Arming clients with statistics encourages them to trust non-traditional options *if* the data supports it. Rather than work gravitating to habitual locations in a relatively unscientific manner, statistics provide a true comparator of competence and open the market to a greater variety of competition. Data facilitates disruption. New players get a fair chance to compete. The playing field levels. Now, possibly, there may be those who voice concern over this. However, such perspectives usually emanate from those afraid of increased competition, and we, as objectively-minded lawyers, must therefore view such opinions warily.

Data facilitates disruption.

Unprofessional?

Lawyers might also be concerned that reference to objective data is uncouth and unprofessional, like "*Moneyball*" for lawyers. I disagree. Referencing statistics can be done entirely gracefully. We have seen it above. Below is another example, this time emphasising an overall team result:[20]

Announcement

We are pleased to announce that a study of Supreme Court decisions in the last three years reveals [Our Firm] recorded the highest 'win' rate for firms with ten or more appearances.

---

20 With thanks to a former colleague and his graceful social media announcement, which I have used and modified by way of example.

Our Firm – Won 15 of 17 cases (88%)

Law Firm 2 – Won 13 of 19 cases (68%)

Law Firm 3 – Won 11 of 19 cases (57%)

Law Firm 4 – Won 8 of 18 cases (44%)

A massive congratulations to all our lawyers involved in obtaining this wonderful outcome. Of course, while numbers (and 'wins') are not everything, they demonstrate [Our Firm's] outstanding ability to position matters for success and deliver results when they are needed most.

Unprofessional? No. Uncouth? Hardly. Convincing? Yes, very much so!

In a sea of undifferentiated legal providers, all claiming to be the "best", "market-leading", or "pre-eminent", such data provides the client with a level of convincing evidence to equip them to make a meaningful and sensible selection between lawyers.

Objections

That's not to say all objections to statistics are invalid. There are some potential downsides.

Like any measurement, they will be gamed, if allowed. Refusing to take on low-prospect cases to keep your 'win rate' high is the most obvious example. This potentially puts many deserving litigants beyond the court's assistance (history is full of important cases that win, despite all initial predictions to the contrary).

Also, knowing results are closely watched, lawyers may drive inappropriately hard to win at all costs. This may conflict with a client's preference to win, but not at any expense. Or it may temp unethical behaviour in privileging victory above all.

Some may also say that my data is unflattering. Of course, that is no excuse at all and should be a spur to improve it (either at an individual level or as a team).

Other problems can no doubt be hypothesised. But we must beware of babies and bathwater. Statistics *do* help. The key is to consume them not unthinkingly but discerningly. A lawyer with a high win rate might be artificially inflating it. In contrast, a lawyer with a low win rate may have a good reason. We can probe gently to reveal more of the true story that always sits behind the numbers. *"Why is your win rate so low? Well, I always act for the underdog"*. Fair enough!

Otherwise, by dismissing statistics, we lose a helpful, fair, impartial guide to competence in favour of what we currently have. Haircuts.

Conclusion

Many lawyers claim to be the "best", but quite hypocritically, given the nature of our profession, they are often reluctant to provide actual evidence to prove it.

Data provides a solution. What would you want to know if you had to select a basketball player to take a free-throw shot for you worth a million dollars? Of course, how many free throws have you made?

Not particularly:

- Who do you play for?
- Which shoes do you wear?
- Do I know you?
- Do you have nice hair?
- Did you go to my university?
- Did you make a free throw once, which was made into a film?
- How much do you charge per free throw?
- Do you look like a basketballer?
- How long have you been shooting free throws?
- How nice is your car?
- How many times have you been photographed in the media?

None of this is in any way relevant! We just want to know: how many free throws have you made in your career? What's your percentage? 975 out of

1000? You're hired! 40 out of 100? No thanks!

We need to look no further for the most relevant and convincing evidence of competence in a lawyer. And while statistics in an unpredictable forum like litigation (unlike the basketball court) are never the full story, they are a very convincing start.

Absent objective data, we never escape from the echo chamber of constantly debating "*who is better*" without any means of driving that discussion to a conclusion. It will always be a futile debate that reinforces the hierarchy of the status quo – if I cannot *prove* the new firm is better, safety, security and habit mean I should simply hire the most expensive one I can afford.

It's time to gracefully retire this methodology for selecting a lawyer. Single cases, looks, and cost are irrelevant, and we should move past the era of gut feel and traditional providers. This century is increasing the story of '*big data*'. It's time we collectively jumped on board.

Just ask yourself: whom would you hire for *your* million-dollar shot? And are you looking at anything but their free throw stats? And should you?

CHAPTER 10 - IN DEFENCE OF THE BILLABLE HOUR

"I'd exercise more if it were billable."

- Stu's Views[21]

Attacks on the billable hour flow freely, yet we rarely hear from the defence. Consider this the closing submission on its behalf.

Character reference

First, the character reference. The billable hour has been accused of being a variety of unkind things, including a "scourge"[22], a "tyranny"[23], and a concept that deserves to "die".[24]

But what do the facts show? The billable hour has served the profession

---

21 Stu's Views, 'I'd Exercise More if it Were Billable' (Cartoon, 2002) https://stus.com/Billable-Exercise-cartoon-cla235f2

22 https://slate.com/news-and-politics/2008/01/how-to-kill-the-law-firm-billable-hour.html

23 https://www.dcbar.org/bar-resources/publications/washington-lawyer/articles/january-2005-billable

24 https://www.abajournal.com/magazine/article/the_billable_hour_must_die

for nearly a century. And from that fact alone, we have to conclude that the arrangement has not been a total disaster. The law still functions, the profession exists, and, given the billable hour's durability, it probably doesn't pose a present and immediate risk to the rule of law.

Hence, allegations that the billable hour represents a "scourge"[25] or a "tyranny"[26] that must "die"[27], be "destroyed"[28], or "killed"[29] probably overstate the severity of the threat.

Moreover, rather than being simply passively harmless, the billable hour is actively useful in other ways. It integrates nicely into the way a lawyer and law firm works. In all the bad press, these advantages of the billable hour are often overlooked.

For instance, it rewards lawyers appropriately. Hours worked equals dollars earned. Same as a casual supermarket employee. There is no windfall if the lawyer obtains a quick result, nor does the lawyer work for free if the case drags on.

The billable model also ensures that lawyers are given the widest possible latitude to do what is in their judgement necessary to win the case. It can be an unhelpful distraction to be constrained by a budget in must-win scenarios. As before, the admiral would be less effective if they had to ask whether they could afford to fire a missile, and it is the same with lawyers. The quality of legal representation tends to be curtailed by upfront fixed budgets, whereas the flexibility of charging for all time (reasonably spent) ensures top quality.

And this is not just a matter of "our side winning" but has larger ramifications for the functioning of the judicial system. If the lawyers on both sides are

---

25 https://slate.com/news-and-politics/2008/01/how-to-kill-the-law-firm-billable-hour.html

26 https://www.dcbar.org/bar-resources/publications/washington-lawyer/articles/january-2005-billable

27 https://www.abajournal.com/magazine/article/the_billable_hour_must_die

28 https://www.walkercorporatelaw.com/lawyers/its-time-to-destroy-the-billable-hour/

29 https://www.afr.com/companies/professional-services/companies-want-lawyers-to-kill-the-billable-hour-20170619-gwu2yd

sufficiently supported by doing everything necessary to win the case, the truth and best result will prevail. But if one side is handicapped by a budget such that they cannot commit to the battle fully, we can be less confident that truth, rather than resources, has driven the result.

Clients benefit, too. The timesheet allows effort to be tracked, monitored, and (if necessary) audited by the client. Further, there is also no need for complicated scoping exercises to delay the start of work – the billable model facilitates a quick start, which is often necessary for litigation.

The billable hour also avoids the connotation of "low quality' which attaches to a fixed fee. As homeowners plagued with a defective home know, a fixed fee encourages (from builders and others) cutting corners to maximise profits. Hence, the model struggles to shake the perception of being a budget option. No such concern exists with the billable model. The most pressing risk with the billable model is that clients will get "too much quality" through over-servicing, which is, for many clients, less problematic than the low-quality inverse.

Even internal law firm management is facilitated by the billable hour. Finding an objective way to measure a lawyer's performance is difficult, and it is often difficult to objectively assess the relative merit of lawyers internally. While a ranking scale relative competence might be achievable, it is difficult to say, for instance, whether a lawyer has met the required standards of quality in isolation.

The billable targets imposed on lawyers provide a shortcut. Assuming that lawyers who please their internal clients receive more work, the busiest lawyers will be the best, most popular lawyers. So instead of having to collate impressionistic, non-objective measures of quality from a large number of internal clients, all the firm has to ask is, "who is busiest"? The stars will be popular and at full capacity, while the less-than-stellar performers will struggle to meet targets. The old saying that "*bad lawyers don't get fired, they just stop receiving work*" applies with equal force internally as externally.

Criticisms

But we need not defend the billable hour only by background character references. We can also rebut the specific allegations of wrongdoing.

They boil down to three:

- Destroys work-life balance
- Encourages padding the bill
- Rewards inputs over outputs

Time to respond.

Allegation One: Destroys Work-Life Balance

> *For too many litigators, our life increasingly is a highly paid serfdom—a cage of relentless hours, ruthless opponents, constant deadlines and merciless inefficiencies.*
>
> *Scott Turlow*
>
> *The Billable Hour Must Die.*[30]

The first criticism is that billable hours destroy a lawyer's work-life balance. When the billable hour was first introduced, it was suggested that lawyers aim for 1300 hours a year. Still, by slow accretion, these targets per lawyer have increased to more than 2000 in many of the largest firms. When hard time drives out soft, this means lawyers spend longer at work than they do at home, causing, it is said, increasing levels of fatigue and misery in the profession.

As the attorney for the defence, I challenge this. First, not all firms require 2000 hours. But even taking that figure, working 2000 hours a year equates to about 9 hours a day, only one hour more than the labour movement secured

30 https://www.abajournal.com/magazine/article/the_billable_hour_must_die

worldwide starting in the 1850s. This is hardly a crushing chunk of time, especially considering how well lawyers are paid, and compares favourably to the hours worked by other professionals, ER doctors, CEOs, investment bankers and alike.

Moreover, there is a more fundamental point to be made. It's never the time. It's the enjoyment.

It's never the time. It's the enjoyment.

Before I was a lawyer, I had two part-time jobs. One was working at a reception centre, waiting tables for weddings and large functions as one of the armies of black-aproned waiters. Shifts lasted eight hours or so from 5 pm to 1 am, and we were on our feet for most of the time, aside from a 15-minute break to eat some complementary leftover food from the kitchen for dinner. It was long, physical, tiring hard work, and the time passed at a snail's pace. I could bear, at most, to do this twice a week (max).

My other job was as an educational and motivational speaker to high school students. I would speak to groups about the importance of time management, goals and discipline in their studies.

This speaking job was very different. Shifts would last nominally about four hours as I left home, drove to a school and presented, chatted with students afterwards and then drove home. Yet because the work was exciting, rewarding and thrilling (public speaking always is), those four hours flew. I could have easily (and often did) packed multiple sessions into a day and a week. And while not without its challenges and annoyances, it didn't feel like work for the most part.

Hypothetically, if I worked full time at the reception centre, I would have most likely bitterly complained that "I work too much". On the other hand, even six-day-a-week employment as a motivational speaker would barely register as problematic to my mind. I was well-paid and motivated and genuinely enjoyed most of it.

To further illustrate. The other activity that took up much time before I was a lawyer was computer gaming. In a terrible case of misspent youth, I spent up to nine hours playing computer games at a time in and around my other study and work commitments. And did I ever complain? No! I loved it!

I reiterate my comment from these comparisons – it's not the time. It's the enjoyment. When lawyers complain that 9 hours of work a day destroys their work-life balance, they actually are saying, "*I don't like my job*". Nobody ever complains that their nine-hour fishing trip, lazy Sunday afternoon at the pub, or day of golf impinges on the "*balance*" of their life. No one who enjoys what they are doing complains about doing it for nine hours daily. They'll want to do more of it!

Complaints about a lack of work-life balance inevitably reveal, in the fact of the complaint itself, the real problem. The lawyer is not enjoying the work. And the work will not change simply because you change the foundation on which you bill the client.

Allegation Two: Facilitates misuse

"The shortcomings of hourly billing are well illustrated by an anecdote involving my daughter. When she was 12, she asked me for a summer job. I needed some administrative work, and she agreed to take on the task. She asked me how much I intended to pay her, and I responded, unreflectively, that I thought I would pay her a certain amount per hour. She thought about that for a few seconds, smiled and then said, 'Well, I'll take my time then.' Suppose a 12-year-old can see the shortcomings of hourly billing. In that case, it puzzles me that major international corporations cannot also see the problem here."

Richard Susskind
Tomorrow's Lawyers

The argument is essentially that because the billable hour *could* be misused, it should not be used at all. This criticism also lacks substance.

Now, it is readily conceded that the billable hour has the potential to be misused. Any cost-plus model does. But in life, many things could be misused and are not disallowed for that reason alone. Cars, knives and fire. Baseball bats, tin hats and an old tyre. In fact, there is little out there in the world that could *not* be put to evil if someone was especially compelled to do the wrong thing.

Yet, we do not issue blanket bans on all these everyday items. The approach must be more nuanced when items can have both legitimate and illegitimate uses, as with the billable hour.

Computers are a good example. They are equally capable of good and evil. Yet when a single rogue uses a computer to hack into a bank account, there is no collective call for everyone else to hand back their PCs. That would be a sledgehammer to crack a walnut, depriving many of a useful tool because of the irresponsible actions of one. In the same vein, we do not insist that all drivers hand in the keys every time someone speeds and causes a crash, chefs hand back their knife sets whenever someone is stabbed, or ban chocolate when someone overeats and develops diabetes.

Instead, we blame and punish (or help) the individual. Not the tool. The tool is just a thing, blameless, merely the facilitating medium. This means if there are instances where a lawyer uses the billable hour to overcharge a client, we should reprimand and punish the lawyer, not the hapless fiscal arrangement that was unwillingly co-opted into the crime.

Because as mentioned above, there are useful aspects of the billable hour. Convenience. Ease. Transparency. And we shouldn't deprive the honest majority of these useful features because of the actions of the irresponsible few.

Charge 3: Rewards inputs over outputs

> *You don't get paid for the hour. You get paid for the value you bring to the hour.*
>
> *Jim Rohn*

The final charge levelled at the billable hour is that it rewards lawyers solely for the cost of their inputs (their time), not the value of their outputs. In short, lawyers are rewarded for activities, not results.

The point of such criticism is that it would be fairer if lawyers charged for the *value* they delivered to their clients than for the volume of activity undertaken.

Superficially, this seems attractive. Yet, as counsel for the defence, we must point out several intractable difficulties with this reasoning.

Can litigation lawyers really deliver value?

The first difficulty is, of course, how do you determine *value*? And is this a fair expectation for litigation lawyers to do so? Arguably, litigators simply assist in enforcing a legal right. It is in this legal right that any value exists. Litigation lawyers, therefore, do not (and cannot) generate value. They merely assist in unlocking it.

Therefore, charging based on the value rendered seems theoretically problematic, if not practically impossible.

Do you actually want value billing?

And even if the theory could be overcome, and a fee charged based on value delivered, the second objection is this: when push comes to shove, do you want value-based billing?

In some instances, it may work. But not always. For instance, if we were to adopt 'value-based' billing, the following anomalies would occur and have to be accepted:

- A lawyer who achieves a $1 million settlement after one hour of work could plausibly charge $500,000;
- A lawyer who works for an entire year for a defendant who dramatically admits liability in court gets paid $0;
- Two lawyers charge different fees for the same work – the large defendant values the litigation very little, so pays only a nominal fee. In contrast, the plaintiff (who has been crippled by an accident) values the same litigation very highly. Hence, the lawyer charges a commensurately higher fee.

These are the uncomfortable realities attendant upon adopting a 'value-based' model. Value, to the extent it can be identified, is dynamic and in the eye of the beholder. For better or worse, lawyers and society would have to accept a similar fluctuation in lawyers' remuneration. And as the examples above show, from an optics perspective, this can operate perversely.

In the above circumstances, what is fairer? An hourly model. The lawyer who achieves a quick and fast settlement is paid for their time, not a windfall. Same for the hardworking but unlucky defence lawyers – they are not left with anything. A value-based model sounds superficially attractive, but the practical realities of its wholesale adoption pose some intractable difficulties.

It's already done

Finally, the free market exists on the assumption that a bargain freely struck between two rational economic actors creates value for both sides.

If we accept this conclusion, which indeed we must if we are to adhere to centuries of economic orthodoxy, it follows inevitably that we already exist in a value billing model. If a billable arrangement did not represent "value" to the client, they would not engage our services on these terms. They would seek alternative terms. In a world where we are all rational economic beings, all seeking our own economic advancement, we have to conclude that by the mere virtue that the client has voluntarily entered the billable hour arrangement, it represents a "value" to them.

To do otherwise would be to disrupt the market by saying, with a degree of arrogance, 'you are not able to determine what is of value to you'.

With respect, the market and its participants are best placed to identify their own conception of value. And if they are willing, they enter a billable arrangement because they find value in it. Banning the billable hour does not ensure that value is delivered. Instead, it does the opposite. Cutting clients off from a deal they otherwise want cuts them off from a source of value and, for all practical purposes, destroys it.

Healthy urgency – The solution[31]

As defence counsel, I would also like to point out that complaints about the billable hour don't emanate from the arrangement itself but rather often from how it is managed.

All complaints about the model will melt away if managed correctly, and that is by creating a sense of healthy urgency in the lawyer's work.

Create a sense of urgency in legal work, and these complaints about the billable hour melt away.

Imagine the following common scenario. It is the day before the Christmas break up, and you are due at the airport at 8.00 pm. You come in at 8.30 am and survey the day's work ahead of you. It's a full deck. You immediately get started. You work quickly and efficiently, knowing that you must fit everything into a compressed timeframe. In your professional judgment, you jettison activities that are perhaps justifiable but not strictly necessary to produce the deliverable. You delegate appropriately and as necessary. Each hour you spend on the task is an hour well spent and truly worth your charge-out rate. You

31 This section draws on the observation that a professional services firm works best when slightly *overworked* from "Maister, David H. Managing the Professional Service Firm. 1997".

push yourself, move quickly from task to task, look up at the end of the day having completed all your work, and are billed 9 hours by 5.30 pm with time to spare. You shut down your computer and head to the airport, feeling satisfied with a job well done.

This is a situation where the billable hour has worked well. The lawyer has been given a significant amount of professional latitude to produce a deliverable (which is often impossible in a more proscriptive fixed fee model). However, there has not been any "defensive lawyering", "padding", "overcharging or "paying for activity rather than results", which is so often said to be the second vice of the billable model (Allegation 2: Potential for misuse). The time pressure placed on the lawyer has meant there has not been time for the lawyer to engage in these less-than-productive activities.

In addition, the lawyer is unlikely to have felt "strapped to the clock", performing excessive amounts of work at the expense of their "work-life balance" to achieve astronomical billable targets (Allegation 1: Destroys work-life balance). On the contrary, conquering the urgent but achievable tasks of the day has probably left them with a satisfied glow of professional satisfaction *and* allowed them to go on holiday.

Finally, with the lawyer working energetically and efficiently, the clients will likely receive a good quality work product for a fair price – a very attractive value proposition. Hence, as this represents good value, there is no need to superimpose an additional 'value-based billing' model over the existing arrangement (Allegation 3: Value-based billing is fairer).

In short, a bit of healthy urgency, a slight stretch goal, and the right about of challenge is the appropriate managerial culture to create to allow the billable hour to show its strength. If that is lacking, it is not the remuneration model which is to blame.

Conclusion

Members of the jury, to conclude. In a profession everyone loves to hate, the "billable hour" has become a convenient, visible and easily comprehensible scapegoat around which diffuse streams of criticism can coalesce.

Yet, as we have seen, the billable hour has robustly weathered the storm of these criticisms, and for a good reason. It has clear advantages. And the purported disadvantages do not stand up to scrutiny.

We can have confidence that the criticism lacks merit because of a further simple observation: lawyers operate in a free market. Clients have a choice, the option, and the power to ask for a different billing arrangement if they want it. Overwhelmingly, they do not. The only conclusion we can draw from this is that the billable hour remains acceptable to the one entity entitled to arbitrate the issue – the client.

Clients are rational economic beings, not children. If they continue to pay lawyers on a billable basis, we should not, in our hubris, try to displace that free choice through paternalistic intervention and attempts to ban the billable hour for its perceived (but debunked) evils.

Such an attack on freedom of economic choice is a veiled attack on freedom itself.

I leave you to your deliberations.

CHAPTER 11 - A FIXED FEE?

"Doubt is not a pleasant condition, but certainty is an absurd one."

-Voltaire (1694 – 1778)

The obvious downside to the billable model is that it lacks price certainty for the client. Bill shock is a real and present danger.

If money is no object, this is no objection. But there are plenty of cases where the client does want to balance the need to win with the need to stay under budget. Why does a fixed fee remain so uncommon in these instances?

The answer illustrates the old adage: it's easy to identify problems but hard to make solutions work. The simple reality is that collectively, as a profession, we have not found a way to make a fixed fee consistently work.

Of course, there are professional pockets where the fixed fee exists happily. Yet the *systemic* adoption of a fixed fee to displace the billable hour at an industrial level has been elusive.

Let's examine why.

The pre-conditions

In order for all litigation lawyers to charge a fixed fee, they must be able to calculate, in advance, how much the case will cost to run.

When we boil the options down to their simplest formulations, we can see there are only two ways to achieve this.

1. Use the average cost from many similar cases in the past, or
2. plan the litigation carefully upfront.

If lawyers widely adopted either of these options, we would see a far greater prevalence of work performed using a fixed fee. Unfortunately, history tells us that neither of these options is as easy to implement as they first appear.

Averages

The first option is to use averages. When the firm has done a sufficiently high volume of homogenous cases from which a statistically valid mean can be calculated, it enters the realm of being able to charge a fixed fee.

It can say:

> *We've done one hundred of these cases, and we know, on average, it costs us $10,000. This, plus a profit percentage, therefore, becomes our fixed price. We accept that some cases will cost us more and some will cost less, but we can be confident that it will average out over many cases.*

This method of averaging provides a simple and accurate way to estimate costs. In figuring out how much to charge, the firm needs to do little more than look at the accumulated data and do a sum. It requires no change to how the work is performed, no new skills, and very little disruption to established lawyering. It's just division, it's not disruptive, and it's hence very attractive.

Or at least, that's the theory. In reality, making this methodology work requires a few further pre-conditions, and these are not always widely available:

1. Common cases
2. Uncommon lawyers
3. Confident firms

Common cases

A fixed fee methodology can only be used when a sufficient volume of similar cases allows a sensible average to be derived.

Some types of cases occur in great volumes, arising from the types of situations that happen all the time. Car accidents. Disputed wills. Petty thefts. There are (for instance) thousands of workplace injury disputes yearly, and a fixed fee can be sensibly extracted from the available costing data.

But there are also plenty of entirely unique cases, never before or to be seen again. Ordinance explosion on a military vessel. A corruption investigation into a sitting president. Constitutional challenge to same-sex schools.

Calculating a fixed fee based on historical averages is impossible for these uncommon disputes. There is simply no data; without this, the necessary average cannot be derived.

This means a fixed fee based on "simple division" is never going to be to apply to all types of cases. When cases are common, it's fine. But uncommon cases, which are one of a kind, unusual and otherwise unique, will always be impervious to attempts to calculate a sensible average based on non-existent prior data.

Uncommon lawyers

So "maths" is not a global solution. A further challenge is finding the lawyers to do this commonly occurring work.

To calculate a fixed fee, a firm must do the same type of case over, over, over, and over again. The firm must be focused. And while pumping out the same case over and over results in increasing price certainty, such monotony is not the preference of most lawyers.

Most lawyers want variety, growth and constant new challenges. The sentiments are easy to spot: "*I love the variety*". "*My firm is fantastic at exposing me to new opportunities and growth experiences*". "*I could never work in a job where I crunched out the same thing day in and day out*". These are all wonderful attitudes, and I share them.

But this leads to a fundamental incompatibility. The firm wants to be focused. The lawyer wants variety. Rarely is this tension well navigated.

Instead, what usually happens is lawyers' (who ultimately dictate what work the firm will do) pent-up energy for *variety*, *growth,* and *challenge* inevitably results in the firm doing a wide variety of work. This diversification delivers the "*variety*" lawyers crave but is devastating to any attempt to derive sensible average costings. When every case is widely different, taking the *"average"* becomes meaningless.

Confident firms

Finally, fixed fees require confidence. To make fixed fee work, you must narrowly specialise on one type of case, saying "no" to everything else.

This requires confidence. To decline now, you have to be sure about the abundance on its way in the future. And it's been frequently observed that law firms don't have this collective level of self-esteem.[32]

Imposter syndrome, the feeling that I'm actually hopeless at law permeates our entire working lives. The imposter constantly worries about being found out, clings to every opportunity for remunerative work, and lacks the confidence to say no and be discerning. We say "yes" at the merest provocation and jump at the opportunity to do anything for any client.

But when we say yes to everything, we end up with a menagerie. A zoo of disputes. Again, the firm's quest for mathematical purity has been dashed, this time scuppered by its own insecurity.

---

32 Maister, David H. Managing the Professional Service Firm. 1997.

Conclusion

From this discussion, we can see that "taking the averages", while simple and accurate, is limited in scope. It only works in common cases if firms can suppress lawyers' need for variety and have the confidence to say no. And while there are instances of law firms that can galvanise these pre-conditions and successfully charge a fixed fee, it is not a universal solution.

Planning

"Taking the average" relies on the past. In our effort to calculate a fixed fee, the other option is to look to the future. In this situation, we try and *predict* the costs associated with a case, just like a builder estimating the cost of a bridge, dam or skyscraper.

While difficult to execute, the concept is simple enough to understand. Estimation simply requires working back from the ultimate deliverable (a presentation to a court) and scientifically calculating the cost of performing each preceding step.

Unfortunately, this approach is also mired with practical barriers in addition to the attendant mathematical complexity.

No willingness to consider

The first problem is attitudinal. Lawyers often refuse even to consider the possibility of estimating the costs of running a case upfront. The objection is inevitable: *"litigation is uncertain – it's impossible to estimate"*.

There is undoubtedly much uncertainty in litigation, but the factor is overplayed. Many things in commercial life are as, if not more, uncertain than litigation but are still performed to a fixed price.

Take construction. On a complicated bespoke project, builders have to deal with the uncertainty of (non-exhaustively) bad weather, union strikes, unknowable ground obstructions (rocks, relics or old rebar), fluctuations in labour and material rates, changes in government regulations, damage to equipment, workplace injuries, leakage of hazardous materials, subcontractor insolvency, changes in design requested by the owner and natural disasters (fires, flood and pandemics). The list, of course, can and does continue.

Yet builders do not simply throw up their hands and despair. They identify, assess and quantify the risk. In this way, they can come up with a fixed price that sufficiently accounts for these uncertainties.

The real problem with uncertainty is, therefore, not existential. It's attitudinal. It's not the mere presence of uncertainty which renders a fixed fee impossible. Instead, the problem with uncertainty derives from the lawyer's lack of understanding about assessing and pricing it.

No training

This segues to the second issue. To put it bluntly, lawyers are not trained to calculate and estimate risk. Estimations, contingency planning and cost management are sophisticated professional skill sets that cannot be faked.

Again, we need to look no further than the construction industry. In order to properly account for the uncertainties before a single hammer stroke falls, an entire professional team takes months to estimate the cost of performing the work in careful detail.

These are skills lawyers simply, on the whole, do not have. We are taught at university to be doers, to swing the hammer, draft the memo, and research the point. But when it comes to coordinating the long-term efforts of a team of us, such as is inevitably required in large, uncommon cases, we are simply – again, to be plain – unqualified.

This is a common shortfall among professionals. Almost every profession that has evolved from one-on-one intimate advising to large teams working on large projects for large clients has done so without layering in the necessary training to plan and coordinate such efforts efficiently.

No willingness to hire

Of course, there is no shame in lacking expertise in something. We've picked law – we cannot be specialists in everything else.

The sensible thing to do here (indeed, what a fragmented economy of specialists encourages) is to hire the necessary expertise to fill the gap. The singer is hiring a manager. The athlete hires the physiotherapist. The teacher hired an accountant. One profession is leaning on another.

But here again, practical problems intervene, and this time, it often relates to professional insecurity. Many professionals, not least lawyers, have the reluctance to cede control to someone outside the profession. Professional soldiers distrust civilian bureaucrats, doctors distrust non-medical hospital administration, and (most relevantly here) lawyers distrust non-lawyers and certainly do not like taking direction from them.

Yet, in this unwillingness to hand over control lies the crux of the problem. Because for the professional planner to do their work correctly, this is exactly what's required. The planner must be given control and the power to sequence various tasks, prioritise critical activities and allocate appropriate resources. To, in essence, tell the lawyer what to do.

For a lawyer used to having almost unfettered "professional discretion" to prosecute a case in the matter they determine most fit, this is often a cultural step too far. The lack of control feels unsafe. The division of responsibility between planning and doing is strange. And taking direction from others can feel demeaning.

It's therefore not widely done – while there are always enlightened exceptions, in general, lawyers do not pick up the phone and ask for help.

Not necessary

Moreover, planning often feels unnecessary. Planning is essential when constructing a building because the cost of changing your mind halfway through is prohibitively high. The building cannot simply be moved two feet to the left.

But the legal world is far more forgiving. This is a world of word processors and occasional spreadsheets, where revising an approach or completely changing track midstream is relatively "bloodless" – documents can be amended or deleted with very little fuss, and certainly not the massive amount of time and expenditure required to demolish a partially constructed building.

In this way, cases can be constantly "muddled through" without a coherent upfront plan because the penalty for change halfway is low. A bit of extra work. Some additional editing. Inserting a new paragraph.

When you fail to plan a building, you get disaster. But when you fail to plan a case, the only "penalty" under the time-based billable model is a larger bill to the client, which arguably represents no real disincentive.

No time

When scoping the works required for a complicated building, professional builders can take months to calculate and submit a quote. Similarly, properly planning the work involved in a case is a significant exercise; the larger the case, the more planning is required.

But this is not possible in an emergency scenario that often proceeds instructions to a lawyer. Lawyers need to get started. There is no luxury of time.

Moreover, a correct estimation of the required work requires data from the client. A landowner should be able to provide the potential builder with a copy of the plans, drawings and access to the worksite so the builder can assess what's involved.

In contrast, instructions to commence litigation often are provided with many "unknown unknowns" present. In complicated matters, the client simply does not know all the relevant and pertinent information at the start to provide the lawyer with everything needed to scope the matter. They don't know what's there and, therefore, don't know what the end product (the argument in court) should be.

So even if the time to plan is found, it's often useless to attempt planning because the client does not know what they want to have built.

Reluctance to work according to a strict plan

Of course, it is not enough that the work is carefully planned and scoped. Lawyers must also rigorously execute the plan to ensure the work is delivered on a budget.

This is very unsexy. Such fixed and compartmentalised work can suck the romance out of work, one of the primary draws of becoming a lawyer in the first place.

Instead of the legal work being an intellectual journey into the unknown as you uncover and solve problems on the fly (with little heed paid to how long it takes), legal work becomes increasingly standardised, commoditised and devoid of the excitement of discovery. You know, in advance (well in advance), what your tasks will be. You will be drafting this document, containing these arguments, at this word length by this time. No more, no less. Of course, such a disciplined approach is necessary if we want to maintain the up-front plan's validity and make our fixed fee viable. Yet for the romantically-minded lawyer, hoping their role will allow them to roam free and tackle the challenge of the day as it comes, the thought of being confined to the intellectual equivalent of an Industrial Revolution-era Satanic Mill is unsurprisingly unappealing.

No respect for budgets

As is often the case, the issue is deeply cultural as well.

When you think of "leading lawyers", giants of the profession, you inevitably gravitate to those who have worked on the largest cases. Lawyers involved in these cases often work (almost exclusively) in an environment where victory, not budgets, is the primary goal.

Such lawyers develop as professionals in an environment where absolute victory, not budgets and deadlines, is the driving criterion of success. It is unsurprising, given this upbringing, that by the time they become leaders of the profession, their views about the supreme importance of quality over budgets are entrenched.

We are all products of our upbringing, and there is no criticism to be made of this. But when such views are expressed and respected as being those of a "*leading*" professional, filtering down from the top and infiltrating the minds of more developing lawyers, it is very easy for the dismissive attitude to budgets to be self-perpetuating.

Inconsistent with a trusted relationship?

The final barrier to upfront estimation derives from the nature of the lawyer-client relationship.

Fixed fee arrangements require, at the very least, that the law firm clearly define up front what is "in scope" and "out of scope". For complex litigation, there would also need to be a mechanism whereby the costs associated with various events are allocated to the firm or the client. For example, what happens if a plaintiff brings a further claim? What happens if a large volume of documents requires specialised software to review? What happens if there is an appeal? Who has to pay for these eventualities?

While there may be a temptation on the part of the law firm to "deal with these things if they arise", this is not necessarily in keeping with the desire of the client, who may prefer a single fee that accounts for all contingencies.

Therefore, to maintain a fixed fee structure in light of such unknown contingencies, fixed fee arrangements will, by necessity, require an increasingly complicated engagement contract specifying who is to pay for each of the identified contingencies should they occur. An extensive negotiation will be required between the parties, as well as a formalised written contract. The client may need to engage an independent lawyer to advise them on the terms of engagement agreed with the litigation attorneys(!) The entire transaction begins to look more and more like a complex building contract, complete with all the trappings of two parties hammering out a deal (including a proclivity to sue if things don't work out).

This adversarial mindset is not closely compatible with viewing litigation lawyers as trusted advisors. It's much easier to say, *"we'll charge for our time, but trust us – we'll charge fairly"*.

Conclusion

Commentary on the benefits of a fixed fee instead of the entrenched billable hour runs deep and long. While the fixed fee is not without disadvantages, the virtues are plain and obvious: fairer, clearer, certain, and improves the affordability of justice.

In the abstract, these virtues are probably true, at least for clients who favour the budget as much as the outcome. But unless the profession can find a way to implement a fixed fee on a wide scale, such benefits remain impotent and hypothetical only. Those advocating its benefits over the billable hour are simply identifying problems without offering realistic alternatives.

Overcoming this requires that we get serious. Either we narrowly specialise (and let go of the need for variety) or accept the new skills and mindset required to estimate properly. Doing either option will work. But it is futile to keep enthusing about the benefits of fixed fees on the one hand whilst avoiding the reality of the required steps on the other.

That, then, is the challenge. To get serious. The fixed fee may be great, and it's fine to daydream about the benefits. Still, until lawyers get serious about either focus or estimation, the fixed fee will remain just that – a pleasant fantasy.

CHAPTER 12 - NO WIN, NO FEE?

"You almost fight against the hope because it is too good to be true."

C. S. Lewis (1898 – 1963)

It sounds like a good deal for clients. No win. No fee! But is it? The underlying economics tell us more.

Law of large numbers

'No win, no fee' uses the Law of Large Numbers. The Law says that actual results will approach theoretical results across many uncertain events (like coin flips).

In 10 coin flips, it might be seven heads and three tails. But with over 10 million flips, it will be almost exactly 50:50. The Law of Large Numbers exerts a gravitational pull towards the expected result.

The law can be (and is) used to make money.

Imagine a game. You win $1 billion for heads and $0 for tails in a single coin toss. The cost to play? $400 million. While, rationally, this is a very fair price, few people would play. $400 million is a lot to lose.

But let's change the conditions. This time: In one *billion* coin tosses, you win $1 for each head and $0 for tails. Same price, $400 million.

Same price and the same stakes. But this reformulation is far more attractive. You *know,* with over 1 billion flips, you will win almost exactly $500 million. And, of course, paying $400 million for a statistically guaranteed $500 million is a *very* fair deal.

The Law's lesson is never to make big bets. Make lots of small bets, and ride the averages.

Like 1-cent slot machines, when players make many little bets, the casino can accurately predict how much they will win in the long term. If it keeps costs below this level, it makes a guaranteed profit.

Firms offering a 'no win no fee' also make money this way. Each case is a gamble. If they lose, they don't get paid. But suppose they have a sufficient number of cases, each with a small fee. In that case, they can accurately predict total long-term revenue. Structure costs accordingly, and profit is assured.

The preconditions

Therefore, to run a viable "*no win, no fee*" firm, there are three preconditions:

1. Lots of cases;
2. Low legal fees for each; and
3. A statistically predictable win rate.

Lots of cases

Lots of cases require lots of clients. As the most numerous potential clients are individuals (not big businesses), firms usually target them. And their needs. Workplace injuries. Traffic accidents. Not complex commercial litigation. This is the only way to get the necessary volume to make 'no win, no fee' work.

Individuals are usually legal novices and unsure which lawyer to pick. Firms must market heavily to attract them and win their trust. Individuals are also usually reluctant to litigate. Firms must be adept at de-mystifying the process and making people comfortable going to court.

Helping the masses obtain justice serves an important social function by itself. But it is also essential for the continued viability of "*no win, no fee*" firms. Of course, all firms must bring in new business. But in '*no win, no fee*' firms, the importance has another dimension. A steady stream of new clients is necessary to ensure the pool of clients remains high enough for the firm to access the law of averages.

Low legal fees

The "*no win, no fee*" firm must keep legal costs (their bet) as low as possible. As mentioned above, many small bets are necessary for predictable returns.

Firms must work cheaply. Automated systems, legal secretaries, paralegals and relatively inexperienced legal practitioners. Fortunately, in their quest for low costs, the large volume helps. Volume lets firms quickly progress down the learning curve, rapidly making fees less expensive.

Again, low fees are a social virtue: the client is not hit with an unpleasantly large legal bill on the successful conclusion of their matter. But low fees are also essential for "*no win, no fee*" to work.

On the flip side, however, downward pressure on costs can encourage unhealthy frugality. To keep costs down, each lawyer in a '*no win, no fee*' firm is often allocated as many clients as possible. For an industry with high rates of mental illness, we should not accept this practice uncritically.

A relentless downward drive on legal fees also means that, in the interests of keeping the fees for any one matter low, there are few "*frills*' outside the technical performance of the work. For instance, there is rarely the level of one-on-one consultation with the client through the life of the matter that the client would prefer (for many "no win, no fee" clients, actual communication with their lawyers is conspicuously absent). This, however, is not indicative of an uncaring attitude. It is simply the weight of the firm's economics at play.

Predictability

You can't calculate your long-term returns if your win rate is unknown. Hence, the third pre-condition to a viable no-win no-fee practice is that the win rate must be *predictable*.

Again, like with low cost, the volume helps. Across thousands of particular types of cases, the percentage you '*win*' (including favourable settlements) can be determined with statistical accuracy. By having lots of cases, predictability takes care of itself.

Making more money

So that's it: lots of cases, low fees and statistically predictable outcomes. If a law firm can achieve these pre-conditions and keep numbers high and fees low, long-term profit is *predictable*.

This is good fiscal health but a bit boring. What about *increasing* profit? That's more interesting but requires some ingenuity. We can't charge more per case because that increases the size of our bets and is a risky path to profitability. We cannot simply get more clients either because more clients require commensurately more overheads to service. This means the only way to increase profits in a long-term, stable way is to increase the percentage of cases you win without reducing volume or increasing costs.

There are two ways to win more cases.

The first and easiest method is to attract *better* cases. Some cases are inherently more likely to win than others. The more a firm can secure its portfolio, the more lucrative the practice.

This leads to heavy competition between "no win, no fee" firms to secure the "best" clients (clients with the highest inherent chance of winning). By securing better clients, profits jump without you having to do anything else.

To get the "best" clients, you need a reputation for outstanding work and results - this competitive tension, therefore, results in better service for an individual client. No social or policy problem with that. Of course, it *can* also promote that sort of icky ambulance-chasing behaviour, but fortunately (to my observation), that appears to be a problem of caricature more than reality.

Happily, the "best" clients tend also to have the lowest legal fees. They are easy cases. There is a happy synergy here with the requirement that costs remain low.

That's option one. Get better cases. Option two is to do more with what you have. With effort, a case with a lower chance of winning can be "polished' up to a higher chance of winning. However, this requires work. Work increases legal fees. Increasing legal fees too much reduces the number of cases the firm can have in its portfolio, placing a strain on its ability to utilise the law of large numbers.

Conclusion

No win, no fee is a unique legal arrangement. The economics can be managed. Balancing the practice's economic needs with the lawyers' professional instincts is more challenging. Lawyers attracted to plaintiff work often want to battle hard for the underdog. But hard work (and high fees) on speculative cases is no way to make money in a no-win, no-fee environment.

How do you square this circle? They say that before you do good, you must do well. A successful, no-win, no-fee firm with lots of small cases should be predictably profitable. And from those profits, the firm can afford to take on harder-to-win and more expensive cases. The profitable subsidises the more speculative but nonetheless deserving. In this fashion, the firm remains profitable. It can claim affinity with the underdog as long as everyone understands the limits.

CHAPTER 13 - REDUCING LEGAL COSTS

"The container is at the core of a highly automated system for moving goods from anywhere to anywhere, with a minimum of cost and complication on the way. The container made shipping cheap, and by doing so changed the shape of the world economy."

\- March Levinson

Reducing shipping costs with containers increased access to trade. Similarly, reducing legal costs will increase access to the law.

How can we do this?

Lawyers charge an hourly rate. It follows that reducing costs requires fewer hours, lower rates, or both.

Reducing hours

How do we make lawyers work fewer hours?

Force

The first option is force. We force lawyers to work less with these hard caps:

- Settling the case;
- Holding earlier trials;
- Setting time limits at trial.

Settling

Settling the case stops all work. A mandatory halt. It is, therefore, very effective at reducing the number of hours worked. For instance, settling a 100-hour case after 10 hours will reduce the legal fees payable by 90%.

Moreover, the parties have reached a mutually agreeable outcome, rather than having a judgment imposed, saving relationships (and appeals).

Such is the settlement's effectiveness. It is often considered the *only* strategy for reducing legal costs. Governments implore litigants to "*Save money: settle!*" But while important, it is not the only option.

Earlier trial dates

If the case doesn't settle, we can set *earlier* trial dates. Lawyers always fill available preparation time. Earlier trials force lawyers to condense preparation, saving cost.

We, of course, cannot be too eager. Impossibly tight deadlines are unfair. But equally, relaxed trial dates cause bloated preparation and unnecessarily high legal fees.

Time limits

The diet doesn't stop at the court door. We can *force* lawyers to save time at trial with time limits.

The court gives each side a time budget to present their case. How they spend it is their call. But like pocket money, once it's gone, it's gone. Use it wisely.

Encouragement

Force is not the only diet strategy. There is also willpower. Lawyers may also *voluntarily* save time with these options.

Technology

Technology continues to replace human labour.

In the old days, the only way to file an urgent document at court was for the lawyer to walk it across town. Or a typing error required the whole page to be restarted.

Thankfully, these days are over. But lawyers should retain the replacement mindset, vigilantly asking: what work can technology replace?

If technology advances every day, every day you forgo this question is a lost opportunity to save time.

Planning

Planning takes time but saves more. Skipping it is a false economy. Without a map and destination, the case will burn extra petrol on the back roads.

Specialisation

Specialisation also saves time. You don't have to '*start from scratch*'. For cases in your domain, you can leverage experience to perform the same level of quality in less time.

Some lawyers resist specialisation. They want variety. But if it comes at the cost of efficient work performance, it is an expensive indulgence.

Reducing unnecessary activities

Lawyers must also jettison unnecessary work. Litigation is not monolithic.[33] Like a building, it is the congealed result of many discrete tasks.

Some require a lawyer. Do those. Some are over-serviced. Delegate those.

---

33 Richard Susskind, The End of Lawyers? Rethinking the Nature of Legal Services (Oxford University Press, 2008)

Some are redundant. These should be ruthlessly eliminated.

Real issues

Lawyers must carry a thrifty mindset to trial. We must focus and present our best arguments only. Because each argument requires a response and a decision, weak or peripheral arguments multiply waste through the system.

A defendant lawyer in an infamously expensive Australian case explains:

> *"[The plaintiff] pleaded a case with hundreds of permutations and combinations literally... They would say, 'we're entitled to run all the points we want to ... and we don't have to, at the outset, decide which are the best and which are the bad ones. The main gist of their case was probably one-tenth of the volume of the case. [But] we had all this stuff around it that we had to deal with."*[34]

'*Dealing*' this peripheral nine-tenths is a poor use of trial time. So focus.

(If not, judges should intervene, extracting the gist from the morass of arguments. Come on. What's this really about? *Really*.)

What is most effective at reducing time?

Hard caps. While they are blunt instruments, they work. Lawyers *must* stop work.

The other options require lawyers to *voluntarily* work less. Whether from a desire to ensure absolute quality or to generate additional revenue, lawyers struggle to stop work before they must.

In a way, voluntary options rely on lawyers' benevolence to do the right thing. Some will, but it is no recipe for systemic change. As Adam Smith observed ago three centuries ago:

---

34 Lawyers Weekly, 'Excess or Necessity? Lawyers Reflect on C7 Litigation' (Lawyers Weekly, 28 September 2007) https://www.lawyersweekly.com.au/news/837-excess-or-necessity-lawyers-reflect-on-c7-litigati

> *It is not from the benevolence of the butcher, the brewer, or the baker that we expect our dinner but from their regard for their own interest.*[35]

Only hard caps (and the consequences of non-compliance) trigger the necessary appeal to self-interest that consistently works.

Still, many feel uncomfortable with the idea of hard caps. In law, time and quality are psychologically linked. More time means weightier consideration and better quality. Less time means work is rushed and substandard.

There are several responses.

First, there will always be a hard cap, in the form of a trial date, to be worked towards. At some point, the music must stop. Even without an additional "hard cap", there will come a point where the pen must be put down. Therefore, we should not be too hyperbolic.

In addition, more time *may* mean more quality, but we need to beware of diminishing returns. At a certain point, the value of another hour of work becomes negligible. Does capping work here really endanger quality?

Moreover, a cap is necessary to drive a finished product. Without the cap, lawyers will eternally tinker with their preparation, falling victim to Di Vinci's aphorism: *"Art is never finished, only abandoned"*.

Finally, hard caps have a wider benefit. It makes time scarce, encouraging innovation.

Consider how you write an essay when the deadline is next semester compared to tomorrow. Or the frivolity of purchases on payday as against the 29th day of the month. And the activities of the idle youth as against those tragically diagnosed with a terminal disease.

When time is plentiful, we tend to abuse it. Conversely, limiting time forces us to use it properly.

Industrial Britain achieved a massive leap in innovation when working days were capped at ten hours. Capital had to be *smarter* at getting more from

---

35 Adam Smith, The Wealth of Nations (1776)

people rather than just working everyone longer hours.

There are always calls for lawyers to be more innovative. But you don't get this by giving us infinite resources. Only the fire of limited time can drive the necessary creativity. After all, if we all lived forever, what impetus would there be to do anything, ever? It is only by virtue of the finite nature of life that we are compelled to produce.

Rate

That's hours. Now, the rate. Demand and supply set rates, so to reduce rates, we must:

- increase the *supply* of litigators or;
- reduce *demand* for litigators.

Supply

To increase supply, we must first increase the *willingness* of potential litigators to serve the market. As in marriage, this is a problem of retention rather than attraction.

It's easy to *attract* people to be litigators. Litigation seems glamorous. Dramatizations in movies, books and on stage portray litigators as knights duelling on the public stage in a noble battle for truth and justice. Protecting the downtrodden. Persecuting the guilty.

But this is a romantic view. More often, the reality of litigation is different. Long hours. Drudgerous preparation. Upset clients, unreasonable opponents and cantankerous judges. For every hour of glamour and excitement, there are ten difficult ones. It's tiring, stressful and never-ending (unless you quit, and many do).

The problem is exacerbated by factors that should make zero difference in a modern world but continue to do so: institutional inertia imposing barriers to those who do not conform to the archetypical white male normative.

Excessive quitting causes undersupply, driving up the rates of litigators who cling on. Clients ultimately pay more for mere fortitude.

What to do?

The reasons litigators quit are far too idiosyncratic to distil universal prescriptions. But we don't have to have universal answers. Just local ones. So ask.

What makes you unhappy? Can I fix it? Can the profession? Which parts of the job do you like? Can you do more of it? Which parts do you dread? How can you give those parts away?

The better the profession is at diagnosing and curing sources of dissatisfaction, the more people are likely to stay. And as night follows day, the increased supply of litigators will reduce prices.

Capacity

Having the will is not enough. You need the way. Willing litigators must also be *able* to litigate.

The problem is that no one walks out of law school ready to handle cases. We need on-the-job training. Experienced lawyers are supposed to provide this, to pass on the trade secrets and tips. But it doesn't always happen.

Why? No one pays them. They must volunteer their time. Moreover, (calling a spade a spade) their self-interest is served by keeping their knowledge scarce and not training others to compete with them. Some will do altruistically, but the masses cannot be fed by the butcher and bakers' altruism.

The misalignment of incentives means on-the-job training is neither rigorous nor widespread. This leaves the pool of able litigators smaller than ideal, increasing prices.

What to do?

The profession must step in. Medicine does not leave the health of society reliant on the altruism of experienced doctors sharing their knowledge (if they have time). When public health is at stake, it intervenes. Rotations. Clinics. Residency programs. Exams. Rigour and structure. Producing good young doctors.

Why? The need is pressing. If there are not enough doctors, people die – today. No such risk exists with lawyers. But *long term*, if an insufficient volume of people is trained to handle litigation, the resulting high prices placing law out of the reach of most people is a no less pressing concern.

Reduce demand

How do you reduce demand for litigation? There is the totalitarian option. Suppress people. Intimidate. Prohibit lawyer's advertising. Discourage seeking legal advice.

But this attacks symptoms, not causes. And, of course, this is unacceptable in an open society. It is better to reduce demand by preventing disputes from arising at all.

How can courts, society and lawyers help?

Courts

Courts can reduce disputes with a reputation for efficiency. Knowing courts *will* catch and punish law-breaking encourages good behaviour.

The following illustrates. My local council introduced electronic parking surveillance. When a parked car overstays the time limit, the system notifies a council officer immediately. There is no escape. A fine for parking violations was inevitable.

The council probably expected this technology would increase fine revenue. But the opposite happened. Illegal parkers soon learned they had no chance. Compliance with the law *improved.* Fines *reduced.* When there was a chance, parkers took it and flouted restrictions. In contrast, when refractions were reliably punished, almost overnight, parkers tripped over themselves to comply.

In the same way, courts that *reliably* punish bad behaviour will improve compliance with the law. Conversely, slow and ineffective courts encourage bad behaviour, multiplying disputes.

This exacerbates the problems of delay and triggers a downward spiral.

Members of society

Just because we have public hospitals does not absolve members of society of the need to proactively care for their health. As it is with law.

The most common type of dispute is a factual dispute. Individuals must take responsibility for avoiding them.

Factual disputes usually arise from disagreements about what was said or done during unrecorded events. This means there is a simple, immediately practicable method of avoiding factual disputes – take accurate, contemporaneous and complete notes.

A case illustrates the point.[36] Ms George underwent surgery on a tumour on an acoustic nerve's sheath. This operation carried a significant risk of facial paralysis. The paralysis eventuated. A dispute arose regarding whether Ms George was properly warned of this risk.

Unfortunately, the doctor's notes were inconclusive:

> *". . .all complications discussed / nat history / csf leaks, meningitis and sequelae. . ."*

What does this mean? Did it mean the doctor advised of the risk of facial paralysis? After a trip to the NSW Court of Appeal and thousands of dollars in legal costs, the issue was resolved in the doctor's favour. Just.

The message is clear. Invest the time to record events and conversations accurately, and reap the benefits when you can immediately halt a dispute arising in the future.

In reality, this is just good legal hygiene. Good hygiene is preventative. You reduce demand for dental surgery if everyone brushes their teeth. Conversely, it's a bit rich for everyone in society never to brush, gargle or floss and then, when the inevitable occurs, collectively whine surgery is expensive! By not brushing, you create the very demand that drives up prices. So don't complain, floss! (And take good notes.)

---

36 *Biggs v George* [2016] NSWCA 113

Lawyers

Confident lawyers get hired. But in their eagerness to get a job, lawyers may be guilty of inflating the likelihood of success.[37] "*Hire us, and we'll smash them for you*". "*It's a slam dunk case*". These words can encourage clients to dive in and commence litigation when a more sober (and honest) cost-benefit analysis would have suggested otherwise.

Every litigated case has one side that is inappropriately confident. It must not be us. We should not prescribe litigation simply because we own the cure. The client needs sober advice, not a razzle-dazzle sales pitch.

Conclusion

The problem of cost is not new. The response to date has been to subsidise expensive lawyers. Legal aid. Or asking expensive lawyers to work for free. Pro bono. Or asking expensive lawyers to defer their fees. No win, no fee. Or sharing the cost of expensive lawyers. Class actions.

These are valuable options. But not exhaustive. In addition to finding ways to afford expensive lawyers, lawyers can also become *cheaper*.

Unfortunately, reducing costs requires the product to be made differently. And no human, lawyers least of all, willingly embrace new ways of doing things. Hard caps. New training regimes. Less trigger-happy to litigate. These are new ideas and uncomfortable.

But the iron law of the universe says that without change, we cannot expect a different result. So, the mandate is clear. And while the steps are uncomfortable, the ultimate benefit is well worth it.

Laws are useless if they are too expensive to enforce. Making lawyers affordable is, therefore, as important as crafting the law in the first place.

---

37 David H Maister, Managing the Professional Service Firm (Simon & Schuster, 1993)

PART 3
WHY

CHAPTER 14 - TIME, COST AND QUALITY

"You can't have it all at once."

- The Hon. Ruth Bader Ginsburg (1933 – 2020)

Every court worldwide is asked to achieve the same thing. A quality decision, in a sensible timeframe, for a reasonable cost. Not coincidentally, these are the metrics by which modern court effectiveness is assessed. However, the tripartite aims of quality, cost and timeliness are often in tension.

In a judicial context, these factors have peculiar definitions.

Quality

While a universal definition is elusive, a quality decision should at least apply correct law to real facts[38] and align with community notions of justice. A quality decision passes the 'pub test'. Not only must decisions clear the first hurdle of being logical, but they must also align with what the community would perceive as fair.

---

38 AAS Zuckerman, 'Justice in Crisis: Comparative Dimensions of Civil Procedure' in AAS Zuckerman (ed), Civil Justice in Crisis: Comparative Perspectives of Civil Procedure (1999)

Time

Justice delayed is justice denied. An unresolved dispute plays on society's mind: a loose end, rambling around our collective consciousness, unable to let us rest. To quell this feeling, disputes must be resolved as quickly as possible.

There is little point in reaching a decision so late the prisoner's sentence has expired, the litigants have died, or the delay in recovering a debt means opportunity costs have consumed it.

Cost

Quality, fast, is tough enough. But justice also strives to be affordable. No matter how quick and excellent, courts, like a miracle medicine, cannot help if cloistered away behind an impenetrable barrier of excessive cost.

Unattainable Holy Grail

While in previous eras, quality was the primary (if not sole) expectation of courts, more modern courts are expected to achieve decisions that simultaneously meet each tripartite aim.

Unfortunately, they rarely succeed. Despite noble intentions, expecting courts to be consistently quick, cheap and accurate is to impose an unascertainable counsel of perfection.

There are two reasons.

Trade-off

In real life, time, cost, and quality are not independent factors pursuable separately – instead, they must be *traded off* against each other. They draw from the same conceptual pool, such that pursuing one drains others. So if you want quality now, it will be expensive. If you want quick and cheap, it will be low quality, and getting quality on a budget will take ages.

This is why businesses tailor their offerings to emphasise certain factors over others. McDonald's is quick and cheap, while a posh restaurant is exquisite for a premium. First class is plush and pricey, and economy lives up to the name – no-frills frugality. Toyota moves the masses in cheap and cheerful cars, while

Bentley relocates royalty in grandeur and style.

Importantly, none of these dichotomous examples (and there will be infinite variations on the business spectrum) are objectively *good* or *bad*. They simply have different focuses and serve different needs born out of reality. You can't have it all. You have to pick. Asking a business to be simultaneously quick, cheap and good is to ask too much. We should not expect anything different from the courts.

Circularity in measurements

Second, we face a quantitative problem. If we strive for absolute quality, timeliness and cost-effectiveness, we must measure each to know if we have enough.

While quantifying time and cost is easy, quality is problematic. Because there are no units by which quality can be sensibly assessed, the law relies on proxies. To do this, the law doesn't measure the quality of decisions per se. Instead, it looks to the quality of the ingredients that go into making decisions.

These ingredients, circularly, are time and cost. Slow, expensive decisions are good. Rushed, cheap decisions are bad.

And therein lies the difficulty. In this inputs-centric model, it is impossible to make a good decision quickly and cheaply. By definition, a good decision is expensive and slow! A court seeking to be good, cheap and quick simultaneously is inevitably frustrated by this paradox.

In light of this, we might conclude that the court's quest to be quick, cheap and good is, while laudable, rather quixotic. We need a new approach.

Malleable justice

The solution is this. Rather than seeking all three factors every time, courts should ensure each case receives the *appropriate balance* of time, cost and quality, as determined by the needs of the case.

This is no more than we do in the real world.

Imagine you are buying a new car. You have done your research, read reviews and marvelled at how far technology has come since the last time you were in the market. When attending the dealership, the assistant politely peppers you with questions. What are your needs? Budget? Timeframe? Do you want all the frills, or are you content with the basic package? You mull these questions and give your answers. Ultimately, you pick a car, dance the negotiation tango and sign the paperwork, driving away a new owner and happy customer.

You got what you wanted when you wanted it for a price you were willing to pay. Was it the best car in existence? Unlikely. But given your unique preferences for quality balanced with cost and timeliness, it was the best car *for you*.

In our economic lives, we are constantly considering, balancing and trading off time, cost and quality to achieve the best fit for our needs.

Further examples are readily observable all around us. Suppose we are constructing a swimming pool for the Olympics. In that case, we will probably want a nationally recognised plumbing contractor. However, we will also (presumably) have the budget to accommodate this and (hopefully) the luxury of time to negotiate favourable terms.

On the other hand, faced with a gushing faucet during a dinner party, we will likely accept paying a premium fee for an otherwise ubiquitous local plumber so long as they can get here *now*.

This balancing approach is the best model for the justice system. Rather than seeking absolute quality, speed and frugality, courts must *tailor* these factors to the particular needs of the dispute. A highly publicised serious crime? Quality first! An urgent injunction? It must be timely. A fencing dispute. Cheap and cheerful is probably best.

Such a flexible notion of justice is not only more achievable, but it squarely aligns with how the real world works.

Challenges of change

But in this conceptually simple prescription lies several challenges. The first is entrenched thinking.

To protect the rule of law, courts have a long-standing preference for ensuring they reach the *best* decision. A quality decision. A Rolls Royce decision. That decision must also be economical or timely is a more recent idea and generally considered (unofficially) of secondary importance. Nice to have, but not the main game, and certainly not to be prioritised over the court's primary objective - quality.

Under a hypothetical model with 10 points available for allocation between time, cost and quality, a court would traditionally assign the vast majority to quality.

Overt manifestations of this mindset are readily observable: *"Some things take time. Justice is one of them." "Justice can't be delivered on the cheap". "Legal rights are inherently valuable and should not be commoditised." "...the ultimate aim of a court is the attainment of justice."*

Despite pushing for justice to be quicker and cheaper, there remain only two ways of doing things for many courts: correctly and unacceptably. Of course, the courts want to avoid needless waste of time and money. But the next logical step, where the quality of justice is deliberately *reduced* to make the decision faster and more affordable, is, to many, unthinkable.

Asking courts to transfer some points from quality to time or cost can feel like asking for a kidney.

Appeal systems entrench this thinking. Decisions are overturned because they were wrong, never because they cost too much or took too long. The unspoken logic behind this is that senior judges expect their junior colleagues to get it *right*. Being quick and cheap is a pleasant, but not mandatory, bonus.

This quality-first attitude pervades the wider profession, too. Law school rewards getting the right answers, not efficient answers. Law firms sell themselves as premium, pre-eminent and market-leading. And no individual lawyer ever dreamed of being called anything but the *best*. Calling someone the *fastest* lawyer would raise eyebrows, and the moniker of *cheapest* lawyer would be a heavy insult.

Our language, too, reflects our attitude. Only *wrong* decisions qualify as travesties of justice. Overpriced or delayed decisions are merely unfortunate by-products of the system.

This mindset is also observable in the disregard lawyers demonstrate towards budgets and deadlines: more aspirational guides within which to achieve the necessary quality rather than strict parameters that define success. In other spheres, delivering quality but at a time or cost overrun would be considered a failed project. A perfectly built building costing twice as much as budgeted is not regarded as a success. But to the law, overruns and delays in achieving a result are simply the cost of business, uniquely tolerated in the pursuit, and as the cost of doing things properly. It's an attitude of artisans not to be trifled with trivial worldly constraints like budgets and deadlines.

In defending criticism of the lengthy and expensive court process, the inevitable response is always: *this is what is required to do it properly.*

To lawyers, therefore, the perennial mantra is *quality first.* Economy and timeliness are secondary. If justice were our car dealer, it would only sell Rolls-Royces.

The problems

Of course, this leaves our car dealership rather one-dimensional. Several difficulties flow from this.

Difficulty No. 1: Not always the best fit

Rolls-Royce justice is not always the best fit for the dispute.

Of course, *sometimes* Rolls-Royce justice is entirely appropriate. Few would argue that serious criminal offences must be tried in circumstances of utmost gravity, rigour and seriousness because these cases require exacting accuracy. The guilty *must* be punished, and the innocent *must* be freed. Society will only tolerate jails filled with humans if they have complete faith that only the guilty are imprisoned. In these circumstances, the tolerance for mistakes is infinitesimal and focusing on absolute quality is sensible.

But that's the point. Rolls Royce justice is appropriate, *sometimes.* Not every time. It is not the best fit for every litigant, just as first class doesn't suit all travellers.

In a less important dispute, litigants may, just like buying a Mazda instead of a Rolls Royce (I had a Mazda), accept a trade-off in quality for a cheaper price. Or a quick outcome so everyone can get on with their lives, even without precise accuracy.

In this circumstance, an absolute focus on quality deafly over services litigant's content with a more economical approach. Paying for quality you don't need or want is not only wasteful, but it's also downright aggravating.

Difficulty No 2: Unobtainable justice

Even if litigants aren't clamouring for quicker and cheaper, focusing on absolute quality can still result in too much of a good thing. It drives up costs, leaving many people unable to afford a car.

Toby was an old, widowed farmer living alone in a small farmhouse in outback Australia. [39] He was retired. His chief friend was his farm dog Tess, and his main activity was walking to the mailbox each Sunday afternoon to collect the post. He would read the Sunday paper at his kitchen table and his utility bills with a troubled look on his face.

Toby had a son who lived in the city. He rarely heard from him, but his son held an important job in a large building and seldom had time to write.

But one Sunday in late November, as late spring heat warmed his aging weatherboard farmhouse, Toby received a letter. It was from his son: he and his wife had just had twins, and they had invited Toby to the city to spend Christmas with the whole family.

Toby was overcome with joy. He had not had a family Christmas since his wife died and his son moved away. Though Toby had little money for gifts, he had saved some old knitting patterns from a magazine. He immediately started knitting beanies for the twins and a blanket for his son and his wife. These he wrapped carefully with brown paper and twine from his wife's old sewing kit.

He packed a suitcase and left it near the door. He ironed his best shirt (not worn since his wife's funeral) and hung it with a pair of pants in his

---

39 I heard a similar story on the television when I was a child. It has always stayed with me. I have no idea what the context or source was.

cupboard. His travelling outfit was ready to go. He counted down the days until Christmas, marking them off the calendar.

Finally, the big day arrived. Christmas morning. Toby woke early, made tea with a new teabag, combed his hair, and dressed carefully. He placed his crafted gifts, neatly wrapped in their brown paper and twine, each with a handwritten card, into his travelling rucksack. Toby was ready to go, suitcase in hand, a smile on his mind. He put Tess in her lead. Of course, she was coming.

He had to organise a car to pick him up and drive him to the city. Next to the front door was an ancient telephone receiver, and the number for a hire car company was tacked to the wall, carefully saved from a newspaper earlier that month.

He called the number. "Quality Car Transfers", a voice chirped. My name is Toby, the old man explained. I want to hire a car to the city. "Certainly", the voice responded. "We have all the latest models of Rolls Royce available. The Phantom. The Ghost. All of them. Which would you like?".

Toby's heart sank. "Oh", said Toby. "I actually don't have very much money. I don't need anything fancy, but I must get to the city today. My son is expecting me. Do you have anything more affordable?" The voice paused a beat. "I am sorry, sir, but we only focus on best quality automobiles. It looks like we can't assist you. Merry Christmas".

Toby sat down on his suitcase, heartbroken. He was stuck. The car hire company, which had a monopoly in his area, was too expensive for him. There were no other options.

Toby waited by the telephone all day. He didn't know his son's number but hoped his son would call to see where he was. He waited by the phone: one hour, two hours, three. Midday came and went. Four, five, six. He waited by the phone all day. It never rang. No one came to the front door looking for him, though Toby sat next to it all day, knitted presents and handwritten cards perched hopefully on his knee. But no one knocked, and no one called.

Toby passed away a few months later. He never met his grandchildren.

When they found him and Tess, he was sitting in his lounge chair, suitcase packed, travelling clothes on, with two knitted beanies neatly wrapped, sitting in his lap.

If you only produce Rolls Royce quality, it's fine for those with the money and preference. But it also means many people will miss out.

Difficulty 3: Danger to the rule of law

That's all very sad, but then comes the inevitable cry: we must protect the rule of law. We must get it right to ensure the law is applied consistently and fairly amongst everyone, maintaining faith in and equality before the law.

This is true. But all good things have limits. A price beyond which they should not be bought, and quality justice is not immune. If we seek it too keenly, privilege it too highly, and buy it at any cost, the resulting impenetrable barrier of delay and cost, cutting litigants off from the court's assistance, leads perversely to the opposite consequence intended.

It forces litigants collectively from the system. While sad on a personal level that their individual sufferings go uncorrected, the consequences ripple far more broadly.

When wrongs are left widely unpunished, like broken windows, it simply encourages further wrongdoing. The link between action and consequence snaps. Justice breaks down. In these dangerous circumstances, the only beneficiaries are the vast majority of defendants who escape punishment for their actions. This is intolerably perverse. But it is also the inevitable consequence of single-minded justice, which too eagerly pursues quality to a fault.

We must avoid the trap. Allowing the majority of guilty parties to escape due to the insurmountable cost of holding them to account not only makes a mockery of our rules but, even more fundamentally, denies the operation of the rule of law, which the pursuit of perfection is intended to ensure.

Consequence No. 4: Depletes resources

Finally, indiscriminately dispensing quality heedless of need or preference depletes resources for those who need it. Judges only have so much energy and attention; they must expend it carelessly.

Consider a comparator. If a doctor immediately prescribed an MRI for *any* complaint of pain (rather than a Panadol and a prayer), we would probably call the doctor irresponsible for not being an appropriate caretaker of society's limited medical resources.

Courts are no less exempt from this than our medical professions. Courts are meant to be healers of conflict, so just as doctors, they are obligated to ensure treatment is proportionate to the illness, saving collective judicial capacity for the cases genuinely requiring it.

Because if you don't discriminate between who needs an MRI and who doesn't, medical resources become overburdened, and those who *actually* need an MRI miss out. Judges deplete their finite ability to deliver quality on the first cases that come before them rather than on the cases that need them.

Quality justice, like any resource, is scarce. It must be rationed with care.

The solution – a new mindset

While these difficulties are troubling, the prescription is clear.

Flexibility. Rather than slavishly seeking quality in every instance, courts must be *flexible*, providing the balance of quality, timeliness and affordability as is appropriate.

In one sense, this seems a novel suggestion and, therefore, ripe for automatic rejection by a conservative profession. But in encouraging courts to embrace flexibility, they can be comforted that it's nothing new.

It's already widely done, subtly. In every country, inferior courts and tribunals of less experienced or able decision-makers are set up to deal with smaller, less critical matters. A small commercial dispute would not (to begin with) command the attention of the nation's highest court. It would go to a less experienced judge. Such delegation is a good and proper use of judicial resources. It is so common that we barely consider its underlying logic.

But in fact, by sending a smaller dispute to a less experienced (and cheaper) judge, we are *sacrificing* some quality to save cost and time. The less experienced and learned judges won't be as good, but they will be cheaper, and because there are more of them, they can resolve the dispute faster. So, as this simple, common, completely anodyne and entirely unobjectionable example shows, rebalancing time, cost and quality according to the needs of the case is already implicitly entrenched in judiciaries worldwide.

Other examples of this re-balancing are also hidden in plain sight. Many civil trials lack juries, have relaxed rules of evidence, and have a lower standard of proof. This increases the risk of mistakes. But it also makes civil litigation quicker and cheaper than criminal trials. Again, this is completely orthodox, and its commonality obscures the underlying logic: cost and timeliness are being prioritised at the expense of absolute justice in civil cases.

And the illustrations even continue to the most everyday disputes. In some instances, it is common for minor criminal offences like parking fines to skip the courts altogether. Some minor infringements now resemble a utility invoice (the ones that troubled Toby so). At one level, it is remarkable that criminal culpability is dealt with similarly to paying our bills. But it's also sensible. The unsaid but undeniable logic behind these apparatuses is:

"Look, society has limited resources. We cannot give every dispute the "A-Grade" treatment. We must pick our battles. For less important disputes, we can sometimes accept inadvertently punishing the innocent or allowing the guilty to escape if the system is quick and efficient to operate."

So, rules already exist to triage disputes and ensure the competing aims of time, cost and quality are appropriately reconciled.

There should, therefore, be nothing controversial about asking courts to more deliberately and consciously balance these factors when deciding how to resolve a dispute.

The Challenges

However, courts will also confront the following barriers in trying to be more flexible.

Safe harbour

Lawyers abhor risk and crave safety. This sets up a nearly irresistible temptation when balancing time, cost, and quality fairly.

Quality is always the safest option. No decision was ever overturned for having too much quality.

With the safe harbour of quality always available, shining its beacon of light to distressed judges in the turbulent ocean of competing considerations, courts will always tend to lean towards making a quality decision. Who can blame them? Being overturned on appeal is the pinnacle of professional embarrassment for a judge.

Spending more time and money to improve the quality of the decision is the tame and orthodox option. It's safe. Conversely, reducing quality to make the decision quicker and cheaper is a leap of faith, leaving the decision subject to complaint and appeal, requiring judges to show character and courage to say "no". No more time. No more money. I'm making a decision now.

With the inherent courage required in the latter option, no degree in psychology is necessary to predict which way the trend will usually swing.

The right mix

Even if courts act with courage and balance quality fairly against time and cost (rather than just seeking quality blindly), we hit a further problem. What *is* that balance?

The answer is both easy and complex. The simple answer is that it should (generally) be in the balance the litigants want. It's their show. The judiciary exists to serve the public by offering an orderly, professional and fair forum for resolving disputes to prevent anarchy. In this servile capacity, it should exist to serve the parties' needs.

(Of course, courts are not completely beholden in all instances. Sometimes, litigants act irrationally. In those instances, the court may have to paternalistically assign a level of justice that meets their needs rather than the level of justice they demand. Litigants on profligate crusades should not be indulged.)

The more complicated answer is what happens (as is often the case) when both parties act rationally and cannot agree on what they want.

This is common. The nature of litigation interest means litigants' preferences rarely align.

The person in the wrong will want an inaccurate trial, and the person in the right will want an accurate one. The plaintiff will prefer a fast trial, the defendant slows (to keep their money longer). Wealthy litigants won't mind an expensive trial, while impecunious litigants will prefer keeping it cheap.

Outside the courts, these varying needs pose no difficulty in the market economy. They can be met. People who want quality, a cheap price or a quick turnaround can usually find a counterparty to oblige. But when two litigants are stuck together in litigation, with differing ideas about what they want, it is a recipe for at least one side being disappointed.

Judges asked to decide how to balance cost, time and quality in their trials face a difficult challenge to reconcile the irreconcilable and impose a process that pleases litigants who often fundamentally want different things. The inevitable consequence is that judges often revert to the safe harbour of quality in conflict situations. If you can only have one, quality is the most defensible. At least it's right, right?

But suppose quality is the safe harbour when litigants disagree on the appropriate balance between time, cost and quality, and litigants almost inevitably disagree. In that case, it tends to place pressure on the justice system to revert to quality again at the expense of time and cost. We are back at the start.

The outer limits of flexibility

Further, while the courts are somewhat elastic in their ability to trade quality for timeliness and cost, there is a limit. Court procedures can only be stretched so far.

The courts have historically been a factory for Rolls Royce's. Expecting them to suddenly start producing on-demand, cheap and cheerful cars is unreasonable.

Even the most progressive and accommodating court is unlikely to be able to meet the preferences of litigants looking for an *especially* quick and cheap outcome to their dispute. Structural barriers, historically and even constitutionally entrenched, will prevent the elastic band from stretching back from quality infinitely far.

Alternative Dispute Resolution

For all these reasons, whilst courts should try and deliver flexible justice with time, cost and quality in an appropriate balance, there will always be a limit to which they can sacrifice quality to save time and cost. So, whilst they should be *more* flexible, we must acknowledge that they cannot be *infinitely* flexible.

In these circumstances, how can litigants who highly value speed and frugality get what they need? Easy. Do what anyone unhappy with a government service does – they go elsewhere.

Unhappy with public transport? Drive. Uncomfortable in a public hospital? Go private. Not disposed to the local government school? Pay for private education.

And if you are dissatisfied with the mixture of time, cost and (especially) quality offered by the courts? Simple. Resolve your disputes *outside* the courts.

You could settle. Or agree, at the start of a relationship, how to resolve any disagreements, thereby embracing the marriage with one eye to the divorce. It is increasingly common for contracting parties to include a clause in their contract saying, "*if we disagree about something, this is what we will do*".

Rather than being forced to purchase the Rolls Royce justice offered by the courts, contracting parties select the most suitable vehicle to resolve future disagreements.

For instance, if they want very quick and cheap but not particularly good, they may decide to submit to a non-binding negotiation. Or slightly better but pricier mediation. Or more formal, costly and lengthy expert determination. Perhaps even arbitration, which resembles a private courtroom.

Of course, these options (aside, arguably from arbitration) hardly represent the best *quality* in dispute resolution options. But that's not the point. The point is that the litigants have the freedom to choose the dispute resolution forum, which is, like our car at the dealership, the best *fit* for them.

Such an agreement works because the parties have agreed upfront on the dispute resolution process *before* a dispute arises. Their priorities have not had an opportunity to diverge (which, as we have seen, they almost inevitably do).

Unfortunately, a prior agreement cannot assist those whose fates collide to create a dispute without any pre-existing relationship. Those caught up in motor vehicle accidents, slip at the supermarket, and disagree about a will are stuck with the courts.

But the reality is that alternative dispute resolution is becoming an increasingly popular means of resolving disputes, and given the opportunity, many sophisticated corporate entities prefer it. Litigants abandoning the public court system and going private suggests nothing less than people abandoning any public service – it is not meeting the needs of those who use it.

This will ultimately be the arbiter of whether the court is delivering the balance between time, cost and quality society wants: whether those who can go, do go. A rise in the preference for resolving disputes outside court should speak with the same voice as any industry where customers are voting with their feet. Something is leaving them unhappy. Something doesn't meet their expectations. Something needs to change.

Conclusion

The task imposed on modern courts is to achieve quality quickly and cheaply. But while admirable, it is an impossible counsel of perfection.

Instead, courts should be malleable. The task is not to ensure all decisions are simultaneously good, quick and cheap but to ensure these factors are in the *appropriate* balance.

Justice must move nimbly between requirements of time, cost and quality. Footballers sometimes have the luxury of time and space to execute a pinpoint, accurate pass. On other occasions, when under immense pressure, anything they can squeeze out is perfectly acceptable. Players effortlessly glide from subline quality to 'best under the circumstances' during a match. Justice must seek to do the same.

To prescribe action is not to ignore the challenges. They are there. But the judiciary must try. We must escape the cage of believing quality is always the best. Quality is *not* always best. If you are ravenous *now* and have to wait an hour at a premium restaurant, you will be pained, no matter how excellent the meal is when it finally arrives. In a desire to place quality above all, the courts must avoid aggravating customers seeking other things or alienating those unable to afford them.

Courts traditionally have considered themselves as a fine dining, first-class Rolls Royce dispenser of justice, assuming it is what each of its customers wants and needs. Sometimes they do. But in the 21st century, such a universal assumption is no longer appropriate. A restaurant that assumed what its customers wanted would soon be out of business. That this is not a risk for the courts (yet) does not absolve the justice system from similar market research.

What do our litigants want? What are their needs? In this case, do we have the right balance of time, cost and quality? Absent such consideration, courts may blithely continue serving *haute cuisine* while dissatisfaction grows, and for those who can, the drift to alternative forms of dispute resolution continues unabated.

CHAPTER 15 - WHO'S ON YOUR TEAM?

"No matter how brilliant your mind or strategy, if you're playing a solo game, you'll always lose out to a team."

- Reid Hoffman (1967 -)

Complex litigation is a team sport. No matter how talented, the "*lead*" lawyer cannot do everything. Inevitably, teammates will have the ball.

Smart clients should, therefore, ask: I know how good you are, but how good is your team?

Natural talent

Good teams have good people. Unlike an industrial manufacturer, machines cannot do the work. We need the talent and energies of individuals.

But attracting good people is not easy – they have options! Cash is necessary but insufficient. Good people are well-paid, but money is not their primary concern. It is a pleasant by-product of pursuing a passion. You must offer more.

For instance:

- Good people want the next challenge. That, after all, is why they became good. Can you offer it?
- Good people want to improve, to stretch their intellectual legs. Do you facilitate this? They want to work with peers. Do you have them?
- Good people want to know the end game. For what are they striving? Is it bold?

Of course, if you can't get the best, that's ok. A champion team does not need a full roster of champions. But it helps. Good raw materials always do.

Training

You play like you train. Even good people must improve, which requires hard work *off* the field.

Training comes in two forms:

1. Structured classes; and
2. "*experience*".

Both have a role to play. Experience is a powerful teacher, but not always comprehensive – your learning is limited to what you have worked on. Classroom learning has greater breadth at the cost of some retention. For most, lessons learnt on the job are sticker than academics.

How to improve classroom training

Cardinal – teach what students *want* to learn. Lawyers all dutifully sat through years of law school studying mandatory subjects of little interest. But as mature professionals, only tailored classes will engage learning energies.

Next, everyone must attend. Being "busy working" is no excuse. Dickenson-era children also had to work instead of study. They may survive today, but their long-term prospects are limited. Skipping class is a slow toxin.

Third, get good teachers. Subject matter expertise is *not* a substitute for teaching skills.[40] Avoid dreary experts. It is better for attendees to remember several points from a good teacher than nothing from a dull genius.

Experience

Experience is what makes us valuable, so capturing it makes sense. As frequently as possible, and in any event after each case, teams should reflect on "*what did we learn?*"

While old advice[41], it's rarely done. More pressing (and chargeable) work often monopolises our attention.

And other subtle barriers exist. Valuable debriefings are not simply self-congratulatory echo chambers. They ask, "*how could we improve next time*"? But it's embarrassing for a professional to publicly admit a mistake, and the discomfort compounds with seniority.

(After all, you must be indefatigable to win and retain a client's trust. Your judgement must be superior when supervising others' work. And if the case has been lost, admitting a mistake may sound like admitting professional negligence.)

So, we skate over mistakes and avoid public examinations. But suppressing mistakes only causes everyone to stumble into the same minefield repeatedly. Obviously, losing the whole platoon this way is less than ideal.

Rather, we must have the courage to be candid. Promoting it requires the debrief to have no ulterior purpose. Frankness will dry up if lawyers feel the admission of mistakes will be held against at another time in another forum.

Individual morale and motivation

So we've got good people well trained. They must also fire on all cylinders.

Morale wins cases. Litigation is won or lost on flashes of brilliance. Those great arguments. The enthusiastic energy of all involved. As Napoleon said, morale is to physical as three is to one.

But morale is fragile and must be carefully tended.

---

40 Susskind, Richard. Tomorrow's Lawyers. 2nd ed. Oxford: Oxford University Press, 2017

41 Maister, David H. Managing the Professional Service Firm. 1997

Wins

For instance, while breakthroughs and progress energise, setbacks demoralise[42]. Sustaining morale, therefore, means (like in wartime) promoting wins and downplaying losses.

If wins don't exist, manufacture them. Every case has opportunities for small achievements to be dusted off and celebrated. Just look! Feeling successful is often self-fulfilling.

Keep everyone challenged

To ensure absolute quality, we often:

- assign someone *overqualified* to do a task, and
- allocate too much *time* to do it in.

But paradoxically, conservative staffing and generous timeframes cause the very quality risk feared. People get *bored*. And a bored mind wanders.

Instead, everyone's work must be in the Goldilocks zone. The challenge is "*just right*". Only this avoids the dual morale saps of anxiety and boredom.

Keep everyone busy

It must not only be the right work. There must be enough of it. For lawyers, being "*quiet*" is toxic. It is not seen as a pleasant opportunity to take the foot off the gas but is viewed with alarm. It shatters our confidence. It plays on our insecurities ('*no one wants me*'). An anxious lawyer with spare time is unlikely to be bringing their best, most confident selves to the performance of their residual tasks.

We often define ourselves by our work. In its absence, we feel lost.

So, to the extent it is possible, everyone must stay fully involved. It is better that nine do the work of ten than ten of five.

---

42 Amabile, Teresa, and Steven J. Kramer. "The Power of Small Wins." Harvard Business Review, May 2011

Teamwork

So, the team is talented, well-drilled and hungry. What else? Teamwork. It always helps to receive a good pass.

Teamwork requires good communication, stability and trust.

Communication

Good communication serves two purposes.

Improves decisions

Decisions are only as good as the information on which they are based. The more a team communicates, the more information gets into circulation. This universally improves judgement. People with all the relevant data tend to show good sense.

Improves coordination

Lawyers are smart. And smart people want to do it their way.[43] This might be defensible as an exercise allowing brilliance to roam freely, but it is not easy to keep track of everything.

Communication is, therefore, important to keep everyone updated on what everyone *else* is doing. This avoids duplication of effort and irrelevant frolics because the goalposts have moved.

How do we improve communication?

Clearly, the team needs to meet regularly. Also:

Close proximity helps. Isolated people do not develop the trust necessary for open communication. Technology cannot substitute face time.

Teammates must get along. They do not need to be best friends. But there must be enough goodwill that they talk. People avoid people they dislike – creating isolated pockets of information.

---

43 Fischer, Bill, and Andy Boynton. "Virtuoso Teams." Harvard Business Review, July–August 2005

Communication should prefer facts, not opinions. Different opinions can cause upsetting disagreement, while facts are inert.[44] We all love to have them, but as in court, opinions should be used sparingly.

Stability

Good teams are stable teams. A revolving door requires ongoing recruitment costs and unproductive time as new members get *"up to speed"*. Worse, whenever a team member leaves, the group must re-form and reshuffle how it works. This is disruptive. Unsurprisingly, the best teams have worked together for a long time in most fields.

Trust

Finally, good teamwork creates trust, an important interpersonal lubricant. A boxer would not enter the championship bout without sparring in training. Similarly, we should not send arguments to court without internally putting them through their paces.

Testing each other's arguments (playing the "*devil's advocate*") requires trust. An artist has their own paintings and authors their own novels. For lawyers, the embodiment of our creative output is our arguments, and for this reason, we can get very attached to them.

Without trust, critique of another's argument can be received poorly. And if we say nothing to spare feelings, our only reward is sending untested arguments into battle.

Recognition[45]

Having forged a great team, we want to keep it. The band must stay together. Recognition helps. Lawyers often miss it after getting addicted early.

---

44 Eisenhardt, KM, JL Kahwajy, and LJ Bourgeois. "How Management Teams Can Have a Good Fight." Harvard Business Review, July 1997

45 See generally Gostick, Adrian, and Chester Elton. The Carrot Principle: How the Best Managers Use Recognition to Engage Their People, Retain Talent, and Accelerate Performance. New York: Free Press, 2007

School, of course, is built around recognition. While tertiary study does not quite maintain the same pace of self-reinforcing congratulatory feedback, recognition survives (there are grades, prizes and internship opportunities).

Entry level, the first twelve months of law are filled with novelty, rapid learning, and minor celebrity status ("*oh, you are one of the new trainees*"). A lot is going on.

And then, the wonderful day of taking the oath of office, completing our journey to fully qualified status. There is pomp, ceremony and limelight. Many people say:

"*This feels like the culmination of a lifetime of study and effort – what a fantastic day. Now excuse me, I am wanted for a photo. A new lawyer is coming through! Don't make me subpoena you!*" [raucous laughter from family and friends, ignorant of the *non sequitur*].

Then, back to work. And then? Nothing. The silence deafens. It's time to settle down and get on with it. The recognition stops.

You work day in, day out. Sometimes, you do a brilliant job; sometimes, it's just ok. But no one says anything either way. Of course, colleagues are *polite*. Mistakes are noted. Clients pay the bill (sometimes). But no one ever gives additional recognition for great work above common courtesy or the hum of commerce. No one hands out awards, grades or prizes.

This leaves a gaping psychological hole. Objective feedback was how we assessed our prior success. Without it, we lose the yardstick by which we have measured our current worth.

So many lawyers wonder – does anyone *appreciate* my work? Even *notice* it? Am I doing *well*? Eventually, completely starved, many leave – ironically, it is only during the farewell speech that the praise flows for what "*a wonderful lawyer you are*", how "*we all appreciate your efforts*", and how "*we will certainly miss you around here*". But the eulogy is too late for compliments.

We must be more proactive. We are all guilty of being too myopic, only focusing on the work in front of us, and not showing sufficient curiosity or recognition of the successes of others. This should change. Even the best teams will fracture if members must pursue recognition elsewhere.

Tools

Modern technology is a marketable point of difference. But do great teams always have it?

Unlikely. Merely having tools is no guarantee that they will be used. Lawyers guard their way of doing things jealously. Unless the tool is:

- Mandatory, or
- compellingly excellent, or
- (most common) demanded by clients,

It will probably lie fallow.

Moreover, tools can only be used by *people*. It is the skill of the wielder, not the newness of the toy, which determines success. Giving me new golf clubs won't help.

Conclusion

The lead lawyer is the captain coach. But in our excitement to play, we cannot forget the other half of the job. Making all of the above happen is our responsibility.

Is it worthwhile? Undoubtedly. The "*lead lawyer*" with a strong team will always beat the captain-coach just focussed on her performance. No matter how good, one alone cannot do it all.

Work is *won* through individual reputations, but this is not how the work is *done*. It's, therefore, sensible for the client to ask, *"I know you are good, but what about everyone else?"*

How do you respond? How good, coach, is *your* team?

CHAPTER 16 - THE STRENGTH OF THE FIRM

"I used to believe that culture was 'soft,' and had little bearing on our bottom line. What I believe today is that our culture has everything to do with our bottom line, now and into the future."

– Vern Dosch

What makes a firm?

The question can trigger several responses. The brand. The history. The calibre of the lawyers. A reputation for excellence through the use of robust internal systems.

But while all these (and other) aspects have a part to play in inventorying the firm, they do not define it.

A unique conglomerate

In reality, law firms are a collection of small businesses operating under a single umbrella. To a varying degree, each lawyer is sovereign and autonomous – they run their own show. The extent to which these individual units combine to form a unified firm, as opposed to remaining standalone enterprises clothed under the same banner, depends on how well the units *link* with each other.

That is, the depth and breadth of the relationships between individual lawyers in the firm define whether the firm exists as an integrated whole. Identifying, cultivating and leveraging these relationships is the real business of building a firm.

This task can be given a variety of euphuisms (nurturing strong relationships, galvanising internal bonds, cultivating networked linkages), but I like to call it for what it is: making friends. After all, marriage aside, isn't this the strongest of human relationships?

Therefore, the short but surprising task is this: to be a strong organisation, firms must help as many of their lawyers as possible become friends.

The benefits of deep relationships

Far be it from whimsical, this is a serious business challenge. When lawyers are friends, it strengthens the whole firm in very concrete ways.

Turnover

Unhealthy turnover due to interpersonal conflict is likely to be low in a firm with strong internal networks.

This results in the following:

- lower recruitment costs;
- less wasted productivity while positions sit vacantly and;
- increased willingness to invest in training (with the trainee more likely to stay, a return on investment is more likely).

Moreover, just as high-turnover firms develop bad reputations (*'churn and burn'*), low-turnover firms develop good reputations as good employers. This is attractive and gives the firm an advantage in the ongoing war for talent.

Low turnover also leads to a virtuous cycle, incentivising staff to work even harder to get along. If you are likely to work with the same people for a long time, you are prompted to invest in the working relationship. That's why we find shared interests with parents-in-law: we will see a lot of each other, so we better try and make it work! On the flip side, in a high-turnover firm, there is no reason to care. Soon, everyone will be gone anyway.

Further, low turnover increases our sense of collectively. Part of what we loved about school was that the cohort remained fundamentally unchanged from start to end. We developed deep, long-term, lasting relationships through the forging of common and continuing joint experiences. And a low turnover assists in creating this same sense of shared destiny. Lawyers perceive colleagues as on a shared journey – rather than a random amalgamation of lawyers bought together by the happenchance of fate for a fleeting temporal period, like travellers on a flight, to disperse after an intense but brief time together. This is healthy. You will likely work harder and be happier if you feel your fate is intermingled with your colleagues.

Low turnover also creates a sense of ownership in the firm. If you are there only for the short term, you won't invest in the organisation. Renters have no reason to perform capital improvements. But if you know you will be there for decades to come, you transform into a part owner of the firm's future, and the incentive to invest in it arises again. Such a sense of collective ownership driving systemic contributions can improve the organisation.

Morale

A firm with good internal relationships should have higher collective morale and energy. That sad feeling of being miserable and friendless at school would be a significant collective drag on organisational vitality if replicated across all lawyers.

On the other hand, a firm with strong internal networks, with a healthy degree of friendships and connections, is more likely to jointly look forward to walking in the door each day and enjoy itself much more until it is time to go home.

Loyalty

Firms with a strong internal series of networks are likely to endear more loyalty from their staff. It is a small step from feeling positive towards the people at the firm to feeling positive towards the firm *itself*.

Again, there are clear economic benefits. Most directly, it translates to lower payroll costs because the sense of loyalty offsets the rational economic agent's tendency towards mercenary behaviour: no loyalty but the highest bidder. Obviously, this must not be abused or used as a foundation to pay staff unfairly, but a sense of loyalty will likely save some dollars in convincing people to stay.

Greater loyalty also prevents run-on-the-bank behaviour if the firm has a weaker fiscal year. Zealot fans see their teams through thick and thin, and loyalty means that when the going is tough, the firm is more likely to retain its essential nucleus and emerge the other side stronger. A collective tolerance for low periods makes the firm resilient to economic shocks.

It also encourages the firm to be reciprocally loyal to the individual lawyers. Quiet periods (to an extent) are tolerated compassionately rather than culled with an iron fist. Rewards are likely more generous and shared without parsimony, improving morale and further endearing loyalty from the firm's members.

Loyalty also has a long tail and usually extends beyond tenure – many of us remain fiercely loyal to long-departed schools – and the lingering echo of fondness is valuable. Loyal alumni may (and do) refer business to a firm, but the greater value lies in their propensity to speak glowingly of it. Such praise is very convincing. It's expected that current firm members will speak well of it: that's the party line. But it is especially compelling when people speak well of the firm after they have ceased having any obligation to do so. So we should ask: are alums complimentary or critical? Effusive or evasive? Therein lies the true test of our reputation.

Improves work quality

Firms with strong internal networks do better work. It's that simple.

Litigation is a creative endeavour, and true creativity – brilliance even –

is born in the nebulous cauldron of human interaction that well-networked firms endear.

When people mingle freely (physically and emotionally) within the firm, chance encounters and spontaneous conversations occur more frequently. And as with combing atoms, this creates a greater chance of a remarkable fusion occurring – the one-in-a-million observation or the cutting insight of the combination of fresh ideas.

Conversely, atoms hermetically segregated are unlikely to collide and cause a chemical reaction, just as isolated people are unlikely to combine to synergise a grand new idea.

We see the same phenomenon in another social science: economics. Higher-density cities are economic powerhouses because of the velocity with which people and their ideas and unique perspectives of the world come into healthy collision.

For this reason, more than any other, firms must facilitate lawyers to "network", to "mingle", and to "get along with each other". It's not just about hiring smart people; it's getting them to mix! A firm without people bouncing into each other constantly is unlikely to ever generate anything brilliant, and certainly, nothing more than a single isolated mind can concoct on its own. This is a waste of a vast pool of latent energy.

Of course, not every idea new idea will or can be a winner. But a firm with greater internal collaboration, by weight of numbers, is more likely to identify an overlooked synergy, conceive the brilliant winning argument, or even incept the next big thing. And to the extent it occurs, firms can take the credit. It has not occurred by random accident but has been cultivated by deliberate design.

Better able to self-correct

Strong internal links also keep the firm on the right path.

With a robust internal network of relationships, people are likely to congregate more frequently to discuss the trajectory they are collectively on as a firm. How's our strategy going? What's working? What could be tinkered with? This empowers the populous. Freedom of assembly is a fundamental democratic right because of the powerful voice it gives the people and the strong accountability measure this presents to our elected government.

Nations where people can freely associate and communicate are less likely to stray in the wrong direction because before this occurs, the people will have spoken robustly and uniformly, encouraging those in power to correct.

A well-networked firm, where lawyers freely and openly discuss and debate "how we are going", provides feedback and accountability to the firm's leaders, ensuring the collective plane remains on the runway.

In contrast, isolated individuals rarely discuss such collective issues nor have the joint bargaining power to lobby for change. We see that power in prison is often abused because the prisoners lack the right to assembly and communication and, therefore, the ability to hold power accountable. Each individual is kept cowered and isolated, and voices of dissent are safely fragmented and ineffective. In this environment, the ruled are powerless to change the behaviour of the ruling, and the unconstrained power often corrupts.

We must not replicate this example. Lawyers need to talk freely and often. A firm where people are more willing to discuss collective issues will more rapidly bring dissatisfaction to the surface. Here, it can be ventilated and expressed by those affected in powerful unison and becomes a driving agent for positive change. This is immensely preferable to the alternative: individual unvoiced disgruntlement leading to people silently abandoning the firm, either in person or in spirit, by no longer providing it with their best endeavours.

If the car is heading towards the cliff, you want the people in the back seat to speak up, not simply tuck and roll.

Assistance

None of us has all the answers, all the time. A well-networked firm is a valuable asset when we are stumped.

A firm with strong internal bonds will likely provide each lawyer with an informal board of advisors ready to receive questions and answers in an embracing zone of trust. It is not the giving of answers the strong internal bonds facilitate (lawyers have no difficulty *proffering* an opinion). Rather the bonds of trust encourage the person to *seek help* from their colleagues.

Suppose you don't like and trust your colleague to respect your confidence, and most importantly, not use your request for assistance as a sign of weakness to be somehow exploited. In that case, requests for informal and internal help are unlikely to be nurtured.

This is unhealthy. None of us is as smart as all of us. If the failure to have a trusted set of relationships within the firm is a barrier to a lawyer's help, guidance, or assistance, the lawyer's performance, and hence the calibre of the representation clients receive, must inevitably suffer.

Without a well-networked firm, each of us is on our own when trying to solve a client's problem. Would you believe you are smarter than the (untapped) collective wisdom of the entire firm? No.

More willing to accept centralised control

The more homogenous the group, the more likely they are to accept centralised control. Federations are always sceptical of superimposed national governments in the early days, and it is only as reduced barriers between the constituent states lead to more homogeneity across the nation that federal governments become more trusted and are granted a more express mandate to rule.

A firm that is ardently siloed with little interaction between lawyers can never develop the collective trust to appoint a leader and grant that leader authority and power.

On the other hand, a well-networked firm that sees leadership as 'one of us' rather than 'a foreigner' is more likely to endear collective loyalty and adherence to the strategy directed by the firm leadership.

More willing to compromise

Deep networks help us all play nicely together.

Inevitably, the decision will need to be made in a firm about which people have different views. To ignore this reality and pretend disagreement will never occur is to be blind to reality.

These disagreements can be handled without courage. Suppose the firm only exists as an uneasy democracy. In that case, hard decisions that require compromise will be forestalled. In contrast, the only decisions that will be implemented will be so lukewarm, so uncontroversial, that they will barely qualify as the strategic allocation of resources that a decision necessarily entails.

This approach would be symptomatic of a firm with weak relationships.

But strong relationships assist us in navigating these divergences in opinion. We are more willing to find a way forward with our friends.

Firms are emboldened, and decisions are more courageous if there is a feeling that a tough decision with which a faction disagreed wouldn't lead to schism and exodus. People who like and respect each other are more likely to *compromise*. Not leave. This occurs because people in a friendship relationship do not have the expedient course of simply existing in the relationship if they disagree. In order to preserve the friendship, they reach a mutually acceptable compromise rather than the alternative: terminating the relationship.

This is how friends navigate differences of opinion (as Obama says: "*disagree without being disagreeable*"). It is possible to replicate this dynamic and the healthy debate in a firm where everyone gets along.

Those extra things just get done

Around any law firm, there is a pile of unloved projects that will undoubtedly make the enterprise stronger and better as a whole, but they struggle to find the lawyers to dust them off and get cracking.

Why is this? A military commander who wants to take a hill can force their troops to do so.

This is impossible at a law firm. Lawyers value independence. They cannot be commanded. Each lawyer will always prefer to do things their way, which appeals to their professional judgement and protects their right to do so. Lawyers are unlikely to tolerate an organisation that impinges too much upon their professional latitude.

But there *is* a situation where people regularly volunteer for projects altruistically without coercion. We've all experienced it – with our friends.

Friends take the initiative to drive projects for each other without requiring compulsion. No law says you must invite people for dinner, organise the fishing weekend or coordinate school drop-offs. Yet it happens all the time (between friends). Just to be nice!

The same thing happens at a firm. When people are friends, those projects *do* find volunteers. One lawyer conducts a helpful training session, another organises the firm triathlon team, and a third travels interstate and reports on a prospective client's opening of a new office. And, low and behold, the needle moves on those unloved but essential communal projects.

A difficult hurdle

Admittedly, it can be hard to just turn around and start making friends. Many law firms are set up in a way that seems to overtly discourage any emotional honesty on which friendship must inevitably be based.

For a long time, the path to success for many lawyers has been ruthlessly intellectual. Good school grades translate into good tertiary institutions. Good law school results translate into good jobs at good firms. Many young lawyers making their way into firms believe the law firm environment simply to be an extension of tertiary studies. I studied hard, got the right answers, and was hired because of it. Now, I am getting paid, and my job (my *sole* job) is to continue to get the right answers. Emotions are for the home.

This perception leaves many lawyers uncomfortable with bringing anything but the intellectual side of themselves to work. Lawyers become one of two things: guarded or superficial – finishing chance conversations with empty witticisms and mirthless laughs. Neither attitude is a conducive recipe for making friends.

Moreover, an inter-office conversation is often tainted with the awkwardness that pervades first dates. We can be guilty of flocking to sterile, task-orientated colloquies, which, while soul-sapping when it monopolies our interactions, at least feel safe.

Of course, there's a time for strict business. But the reality remains, as we have seen, that good internal relationships are an important interpersonal lubricant and critical for the firm's success. Logic and personal experience should tell us that everything is so much easier when you are friends with your colleagues. The firm is a healthier, better connected and more vibrant organisation.

It's also a lot more fun. As an anecdote, I heard once said:

"I used to have a great boss. Every Monday, he would come to me and say, 'let's review the work coming up this week'.

However, he would always add, 'but firstly, and more importantly, tell me about your weekend".

He would always insist on a thorough and mutual debrief on what we had done out of the office, with our families, and our time off, sharing stories and laughs, before turning, at last, to the legal business at hand.'

I think this is a wonderful story. Rather than social interaction being a secondary concern, our unnamed protagonist's boss clearly understood the importance of putting relationships first in the office. That it made such an impression on our storyteller to stand out years later tells us two things: first, it was effective. But, sadly, it was also very rare.

In this rarity, however, lies opportunity. Law firms can become far more successful and enjoyable places to work when trust, faith and amiability are its defining features, rather than just the collective cold intellect of strangers. Given its rarity, a firm willing to encourage and nurture the necessary internal relationship will most likely find it in a significant position of strength.

As the first line of the anecdote teaches us, smart lawyers may be called "intelligent", "clever", or "talented", but the title "great" is reserved for colleagues who nurture genuine relationships.

Practical steps

The firm is responsible for prodding us along like nervous children warily eying each other on Day One of school.

Helping us make friends is a constant and ongoing task because the half-life of an un-nurtured relationship is very short. Relationships atrophy unless given love and attention. And while the primary responsibility rests with the individuals to maintain their link, the firm plays an important supportive role.

The firm must establish opportunities for friends to be made. Imagine a hypothetical new starter. Despite likely maintaining an externally stiff upper lip, it's probably turmoil internally. Overwhelming and terrifying. How is this person going to make a start on "making friends?"

At school, there are a variety of sports and activities that act as interpersonal lubricants to get us started. PE class. Drama. Group activities. All of these encourage us to come out of our shells and connect with others in a non-threatening environment. This is exactly the type of thing the firm needs to do. What social activities can we hold to get people connecting and generate some *esprit de corps*?

The solution is not, to be clear, more "Friday night drinks". These events, I find, given their unstructured nature, are intimidating to newcomers and existing members of the firm and tend to perpetuate existing relationships rather than generate new ones. Attendees gravitate towards knots of people they already know.

For similar reasons, group lunches (another staple 'team-building activity) tend not to work well. People are fixed to a seat, tend to prefer companions they already know, and have no scope to detach and get out to speak with others.

The better solution is any activity that deliberately forces people to *mix*. Like atoms, they need to bounce around to get some sparks! Sports are the classic example (once you've played on the football team with someone, you are solid), and charitable initiatives also work well (in addition to furthering the firm's philanthropic work, a noble outcome). Anytime you can get people "off campus" as a group, it's perfect (for some reason, relationships forged on school camp happen quickly, deeply and for life).

One particular thing I have seen work very effectively is "speed networking". Instead of a standard "drinks and canapés evening", which (as above) tends to simply entrench existing relationships rather than flowering new ones, this has a little more structure.

It was in three parts:

1. Short welcome or keynote address from a speaker on the importance of relationships.
2. One hour of speed networking – one long table, two people sitting opposite each other, a 4-minute conversation, then a bell rings, and the people on one side of the table shuffle down one seat.
3. Follow up with an hour of traditional networking drinks –a great chance to continue those interesting conversations you have already started and work very fluidly. Everyone is in an open and very chatty mood by that stage.

This concept works well (despite the slightly odd "speed dating" vibes the name alludes to) for two reasons. It forces new connections to be made in a structured way, and second, encourages wider attendance because the additional structure makes participation slightly less intimidating for the newcomer.

Who among us hasn't dreaded a standard networking evening where we don't know anyone else? As Nick Callaway says in The Great Gatsby when he first attends Gatsby's decadent garden party, alone and friendless, and is unable to find his host:

"I slunk off in the direction of the cocktail table—the only place in the garden where a single man could linger without looking purposeless and alone. I was on my way to get roaring drunk from sheer embarrassment."

We've all had that feeling, and it's not pleasant. We, therefore, need to make our attempts at networking a little more welcoming and accessible. A speed networking idea, with the promise of the right balance of structure and organic interaction, can be just the ticket.

Measuring what matters

It's also a good idea for the firm to track the strength of the internal bonds. A good practice would be, once a year, to distribute a survey to every member of the firm, asking them to answer the following question: how many friends, colleagues or "I know the face" do you have at the firm?

These categories are not capable of precise delineation but give a useful flavour of the strength of social networks within the firm.

Year after year, a healthy firm should aim to see an increase in the aggregate number of acquaintances. The benefits we identified above are only likely to accrue once the acquaintance stage is reached. I reach this conclusion because you will only take the time to "talk" to an acquaintance or a friend, and nothing can be achieved without the willingness to have a conversation. But once at that point, every additional, even moderately warm connection strengthens the firm exponentially.

Objections

The most obvious objection to the suggestion that firm members become friends is that this is an unrealistic utopia. Law is now a business, and in a business, sometimes, you need to get cross, assert power and demand more to get the work done. Such a power-based dynamic is incompatible with the idea that we all hold hands and tell tales around the campfire.

But this objection is itself objectionable in two respects. First, a firm in which the lawyers are glued together only through the galvanising force of fear is unlikely to last long and, therefore, does not represent a truly viable alternative model to a relationship-based firm. And second, the criticism parodies the task and, in doing so, misses the point. The goal is not to build some fairy tale conception of a law firm: firms are, first and foremost, serious places of work. But there is no necessary incapability between friendship, morale, cohesion and high performance. While you might be willing to let down a stranger, friends *can* compel a higher level of performance due to the powerful motivation not letting them down can be.

A firm of friends does not shirk – it strives. And surely, such a high-performing environment of mutual accountability and support is the epitome of the "collegial" atmosphere we all say we maintain?

Conclusion

As much as it conflicts with our rational minds, the reality is that beneath a carefully polished exterior, law firms are a messy combination of gooey interpersonal relationships. That being the case, the 'firm' exists as the sum and strength of those relationships. No more, no less.

As law firms continue to grow larger and more unwieldy, with an ever-increasing number of remote members working different hours, in different locations, and doing different jobs, it threatens organisational effectiveness. How do you make friends in the modern firm, defined by geographical and temporal dispersion? If, in substance, the firm is just individual lawyers who share similar business cards but without any stronger relationships, does the firm exist as a single entity? If relationships are foundational, and I don't know one of my distant colleagues, are we part of anything collective and joint other than association with a brand?

Such esoteric questions are interesting but need not detain us permanently. The pragmatic thesis of this chapter is that firms can become more effective organisations if they cultivate and strengthen the bonds between the autonomous individuals who form the firm. The caveat is that it is not just about one-time solutions. Relationships take time and ongoing nurturing, without which they wither and die. This means nurturing relationships is a constant, ongoing and resource-heavy challenge.

But if we want to improve the firm, relationships are the foundation on which the firm rises or falls. Arguably, there is no better allocation of our investment energies and resources.

Bricks and mortar may define the firm's physical location, but its essence and spirit lie within the friendships that form under that soulless, physical roof.

If we are (or could be) the sum of everyone we have ever met, it would be a severe waste of resources not to improve ourselves by meeting, greeting and befriending our very able colleagues.

CHAPTER 17 - ENFORCEMENT

"Writing laws is easy, but governing is difficult."

Leo Tolstoy

The key determinant of a country's wealth is its ability to enforce its laws.

National wealth

The formula for national wealth is easy: governments must earn more than they spend.

Of course, as in life, spending is the easy bit. There are lots of useful (defence, welfare, health) and vanity (stadiums, statutes and State dinners) things for government to buy.

The real challenge is in earning! How does the government make money to pay for all this?

Direct commerce is usually unviable: government businesses rarely make enough to meet all national spending needs. Therefore, government solvency traditionally relies on taxation: citizens apply their energy and ingenuity to earn money, with the government appropriating a percentage to spend on the collective good.

This forms the inescapable trinity of civic life: you earn, the government taxes, and the government spends. The entire government business ensures these three factors remain in harmonious balance.

More money

As with each of us, the perennial conundrum for every government is: *how do we get more* cash?

If we accept that national income (excluding borrowing) is dependent on collections from individual citizens, we can express total national income with the following formula:

National earning = Population x tax rate x amount each citizen earns.

Three options are revealed using this formula in our quest to make the government richer.

The most obvious short-term fix is for the government to increase the tax rate. However, as despotic kings of old have taught us, this cannot be relied on indefinitely. The collective rag can only be squeezed so hard before citizens revolt or relocate.

In the medium term, governments can encourage (not mandate) an increase in population. This provides more wallets to collect from. But it isn't foolproof. It requires convincing (1) current citizens to have more babies or (2) potential citizens to relocate, neither of which can be guaranteed. And even if an increased population is achieved, it can backfire if the new citizens are not economically productive and cost more in welfare than they contribute in taxes.

Therefore, long term, there is only one *sustainable* way to increase national wealth: each individual must earn more. A nation of wealthy taxpayers will always be better off than a nation of poor ones.

A smart government must first figure out how to make each citizen wealthy in seeking sustainable wealth.

A smart government must first figure out how to make each citizen wealthy in seeking sustainable wealth.

Creating a fertile environment

Of course, governments cannot assist wealth production directly. Wealth derives from the entrepreneurial spirit of the individual and cannot be bestowed from above. However, governments can usefully contribute by establishing a *fertile environment* conducive to wealth production.

The formula is old and well-known. Governments must establish three key rules requiring citizens to:

1. Trade.
2. Respect property.
3. Not be violent.

Why this trifecta?

By facilitating trade, the government obviates the need for each individual to secure the basic necessities of life for themselves. This is an important liberation, allowing us to evolve from hunter-gathers into a society based on specialisation and surplus. Property rights efficiently allocate scarce resources and incentivise productive work. And outlawing violence ensures citizens can focus on being productive rather than dissipating their energy on self-protection. Society will struggle to advance if everyone must cower inside lest they are wantonly attacked in the street.

So, by maintaining an environment of trade, property and safety, the government lets economic nature run its course. People can barter, work, specialise and live their economic lives safely, earning and accumulating. This inevitably increases the collective pool of wealth. Conversely, if even one of the rules is missing, the nation will struggle to develop and stagnate economically.

"...if even one of these factors is missing, the nation will struggle to develop and stagnate economically."

The importance of this trifecta is also reflected by the fact that it is present globally. Rules regarding trade exist from Portugal as Peru, and criminal laws are present whether it is Canada, China or Cameroon.

Indeed, it is rare that you land in a new country and are completely disorientated by the basic *wealth-producing* laws. The framework is always the same. *Trade. Respect property. Don't be violent.* The sights, smells and sounds may be exotic, but the basic economic framework remains universal.

The paradox of enforcement

But a glance around the world reveals a paradox. Despite having the same basic wealth framework, some countries are economically prosperous, while others are poor. Some countries are safe, while others are overrun with violence. What's going on here?

Natural bounty may explain a divergence in wealth, but not safety. So that's not it.

The answer is actually quite simple. Better countries don't have better laws (as we saw, the laws are always the same). Better countries are simply better at enforcing them.

"Better countries don't have better laws. Better countries are simply better at enforcing them."

Because it is not the law itself but *compliance* with it that provides the collective benefit. When a country is safe and wealthy, it follows as a near certainty that it is also law-abiding. Struggling countries, on the other hand, may have all the natural advantages in the world but inevitably fail to develop due to an inability to enforce the basic economic rules of society.

The simple but profound truth is that it is not enough for the laws to exist. They must be *followed*. Otherwise, instead of a safe society where everyone is able (and incentivised) to work hard and trade with confidence, violence, pilfering, and broken promises will prevail, not only causing irrevocable individual poverty but with a general absence of individual wealth from which to collect tax, inevitable communal impoverishment as well.

The key to riches

The key to national success is, therefore, enforcement. But this raises a further question: if it's that simple, why don't all countries do it? Why do some countries struggle?

The answer is surprisingly human. Enforcement is hard.

In his paper '*What's Our Deal*', David Maister distinguishes between an organisation choosing a new vision, which is exciting, and executing its vision, which can be dull and difficult. In the same vein, passing the law is easy, a glamourous short-term project, while enforcing it is a challenging lifelong commitment. The wedding and the marriage, so to speak. While creating the rule feels proactive and exciting, enforcement requires ongoing (and often difficult) expense, effort and oversight. It requires monitoring behaviour, suing wrongdoers and enforcing judgments – ongoing exertion and expense without a finish line.

It's just like saying: it is easy to decide to get fit. To set the rule. It is much harder to actually discipline yourself to go running every single day, forever.

It's just like saying: it is easy to *decide* to get fit. To set the rule. It is much harder to actually discipline yourself to go running every single day, forever.

And therein lies the heart of the problem. Because it is hard and ongoing, only some countries do enforcement well. These countries, like fit people, have found a way to persevere with enforcement despite the ongoing effort required.

The old days

This wasn't always such a challenge. In days gone by, governments could rely on the putative omnipresent 'God' to be the ultimate monitor and enforcer of all behaviour, with consequences meted out in precise correlation to the wrong in the afterlife. This left the government with little to do. The fear that God saw all and would reward or condemn appropriately was sufficient to terrify citizens into following the basic legal rules, which (not coincidentally) closely mirrored the prevailing religious framework. The Ten Commandments. The Natural Law. Good and Evil. The prospect of retribution in the afterlife incentivised compliance with the law, requiring the monarch (as it inevitably was) to simply (1) allude to the risk of eternal damnation and (2) defer and delegate actual punishment for transgressions to the almighty. In these circumstances, where society depended on religion to ensure citizens behaved, an intertwined link between church and state was not only common – it was essential.

In that era, the phrase "there's a special place in hell for those who break their contracts" was not a humorous nothing. It was a legitimate threat. And it was supported by potent literature such as Dante's 14th-century poem Divine Comedy (depicting a descending and increasingly frightening tour through the various sub-levels of hell), which probably did more for adherence to the law than the immature courts of the time ever could have. Religious credulity forestalled wide-scale criminality and commercial culpability. But this is no longer the case. In more secular (and sceptical times), governments must step in and fill the gap the divine has vacated. Social cohesion in an agnostic age requires the government to enforce the law in a timeous and worldly way rather than simply relying on the abstract and religious to do it for them. Because when citizens stop believing in divine justice, they must observe human justice in action to be incentivised to do the right thing. To the modern mind, the consequences of the afterlife are simply too remote and speculative to have much of an impact on behaviour on this side of St Peters' gates.

Religious credulity forestalled wide-scale criminality and commercial culpability.

The modern challenge

Therefore, enforcing the law is a clear and central challenge for modern governments.

The first step is to accept the responsibility. Collecting and (especially) spending the money of the citizens is the most visible work of government, but protecting the collective revenue stream by enforcing the economic rules of society is arguably the more important duty.

The second step is to expend the necessary attention and resources on enforcement. Given that it requires expense, sometimes enforcement is hampered by a lack of resources rather than an absence of resolution. Enforcement requires both willpower and wherewithal. It is not free. It takes money. If there aren't enough judges, policing bodies and lawyers in society, enforcement of the law will be slow, expensive and hence ineffectual, no matter how intellectually committed the government is to the task.

Therefore, parliaments considering laws have the same obligation as parents considering children: can we support what we create? Do we have sufficient resources to pass the law and maintain it by enforcing it for its entire life?

"Therefore, parliaments considering laws have the same obligation as parents considering children: can we support what we create?"

Without the necessary resources to support the law, it will fade and die like a neglected child. Without enforcement, all laws perish. Not immediately, perhaps, but long term, as the fact that breaching the law carries no consequences slowly seeps through the collective consciousness, eventually even the most upstanding citizen will dismiss the law as fiction. It will be ignored, belittled, and finally discarded as unused societal appendages.

Therefore, if it wishes to make an effective legislative change, parliaments must always ask two questions. Of course, do we want this law? But equally importantly, can we maintain, maintain and enforce this law?

The numbers

This case for resources might be dismissed as yet another cry for "more money". And it is true that everyone asks the government for "more money". But in this case, policing bodies, lawyers, and courts have a convincing claim to it. Their role is central. The courts, lawyers and police, just like personal trainers, are critical to ensuring compliance with the wealth-producing habits the legislature mandates.

The police pursue breaches of public safety, lawyers pursue instances of broken trade promises, and both pursue property infringements, with courts ultimately issuing the necessary sanctions. Without these bodies doing what they do, laws remain inert words on a page and are unable to galvanise any economically prosperous action. Without consequences for breach, inevitably, citizens will stop following the law.

But such bodies are often maligned in comparison with others. In any nation in the world, it is easy to observe large, impressive buildings dedicated to the legislature and the executive. Courts, police and lawyers are often 'tucked away'. But the reality is that few of the laws passed by the more overt bodies, and few of the policies implemented by even the most democratic leaders, have anything to do with '*generating*' wealth.

Government is overwhelmingly in the business and legislates accordingly to (1) *collect* and (2) *spend* money its citizens earn.

The real engine of economic prosperity is those hustling to earn money -

the citizens! And while the government assists by establishing the necessary economic framework (Trade. Respect property. Don't be violent), who ensures these rules are followed on a daily basis, such that society gets the economic benefit of the laws enacted? Police, lawyers and the courts. These bodies ensure that the rules around trade, property, and crime are *followed* and that therefore, society *benefits* from these rules.

Depriving these institutions of funding is, therefore, a very bad idea. Without enforcement of the wealth-producing framework that courts, lawyers and police facilitate, individual wealth inevitably diminishes, and with it, the funds available for collection via taxation.

The importance of the challenge

The rational case for funding these bodies is, therefore, clear. But in a nation with thousands of ostensibly more pressing and urgent spending requirements, the money the government allocates to police, lawyers and (especially) the courts is constantly under threat.

This is a dangerous temptation, for just as in our quest for fitness, skipping a run is tempting but self-defeating. We can see that the total elimination of all funding to these bodies would render the nation irredeemably impoverished. But even more seriously, it is not hyperbolic to observe that the question may become life or death. The consequences of a society being financially unwilling to enforce the law are catastrophic.

Long term, as inadequate funding precipitates a deterioration in enforcement, society will break apart and disintegrate into lawlessness. Of course, this won't happen instantaneously, so reallocating funding to more urgent needs is tempting. But the end game is as awful as it is inevitable. Slowly, without law enforcement, citizens will begin to learn that there is no point in resisting the temptation to adhere to the law when succumbing to temptation and *breaking* the law carries no consequence. They become emboldened in their anarchy. Of course small at first. Who cares? I can park too long without consequence. I can break promises without consequence.

But eventually, once down that slippery slope, there is no bottom. I can steal without consequence. I can cheat without consequence. Even inevitably, I can kill without consequence. This deposits us in the realm of animals, where the only law that prevails is the law of the jungle, where the biggest and meanest prevail. The collective progress of humanity is permanently stunted. Impossible? It's not. It's where a lack of enforcement will inevitably lead. Vigilance and never-ceasing enforcement of the law is the only bulwark between humans and reversion to this state of nature. As the ancients said: Protect your laws as you protect your walls.

And just as walls need constant money for maintenance, upgrades and guarding, so do laws.

Vigilance and never-ceasing enforcement of the law is the only bulwark between humans and reversion to this terrible state of nature.

Good investment?

But on the other hand, while expensive, investing in enforcement pays dividends. Good habits, individual or collective, are hard to establish but maintain themselves easier with time.

It's easy to observe. While law-abiding behaviour often starts as begrudging submission because of the threat of sanctions, with the patient, long-term enforcement, the behaviour eventually becomes collectively ingrained, and habit – not coercion – becomes the primary driver of compliance. This leads to high compliance rates with the law, even if the threat of actual enforcement is rare, remote or non-existent.

Take seatbelts. When they were made mandatory, there was probably much grumbling about the interference of a nanny state with the private preferences of the individual. Compliance would have been patchy and preference-based. But fast forward a decade or so of persistent enforcement, and it's a very different story. These days, most of us aren't even conscious of putting our seatbelts on when we enter the car. It's just automatic and unthinkable not to.

This is the healthy plateau that enforcement strives for. Automatically, habitual, widespread compliance. When society reaches this stage, citizens will pay their restaurant bills, bar tabs and even the roadside honesty box because while they could probably get away with "doing a runner", their habits and conscience prevent it. *"I wouldn't. I shouldn't. I can't"*. As a motivating factor to do the right thing, none is stronger. The fear of a guilty *feeling*, of the echoing heart beating incessantly under the floorboards, encourages good behaviour as long as any guilty *verdict* is handed down.

The fear of a guilty feeling, of the heart beating incessantly under the floorboards, encourages good behaviour as long as any guilty verdict is handed down.

This is obviously a good place for society to be. When conscience and habit replace the need for coercion, it's a far more pleasant (and less expensive) way to benefit from compliance with the law.

And it is a reality within reach of any country. The catch is that it must do the work. Cultivating this high, self-perpetuating level of compliance requires constant, sustained, unfaltering effort. The law must be enforced. Consistently. Regularly. Rigorously.

But eventually, if the course has stayed, results will emerge: a society where habit, social pressure and conscience replace the need for widespread traditional enforcement of the law. Initially, everyone will follow it because of the consequences of not. But eventually, they will follow it out of habit. Therefore, the rate of return for investing in enforcement is very high.

Conclusion

It has been observed that the key to individual success is not intention but action, and the key to company performance is not planning but execution. Similarly, the key determinant of a successful nation is not the laws it passes but its ability to get people to follow them. And for this, enforcement is key.

No society ever achieved a competitive advantage by passing a better law. First, no better laws exist. The winning formula is ancient, universal and unable to be improved on: *Trade. Respect property. Don't be violent.* And second, no advantage, indeed any benefit, is obtained by simply *passing* these laws. Only those countries that enforce these basic economic rules will get results, just as it is the person who goes to the gym, rather than establishing elaborate plans, who gets fit.

No society ever achieved a competitive advantage by passing a better law. No better laws exist.

Two countries, equally in every way, will diverge according to how well the law is enforced.

The dichotomy is clear, and the option is simple. The question is, which country do you want *yours* to be in?

If you want it to be the latter, then you need not waste time conjuring elaborate "New Deals", "Great Leaps Forward", or "Grand Designs". Society is conditioned to look for solutions in the *new*: the new idea, the new framework, the new leader.

But the best solutions are timeless. Establish the necessary framework (*Trade. Respect property. Don't be violent)*, expend the discipline, attention and resources to enforce it rigorously and watch as the financial benefits of increasingly wealthy citizens slowly, but inevitably, begin to flow.

CHAPTER 18 - THE IMPORTANCE OF INCENTIVES

"Show me the incentive and I will show you the outcome"

Charlie Munger

There are two ways to successfully enforce the law.

- Coercion
- Incentives

Coercion

The first option is force. Though effective, it is limited in practical scope.

In some instances, laws can be enforced by making it impossible (or at least very difficult) to break them. Locking your car makes car theft hard. Building walls on the border makes illegal entry problematic. Installing ticket barriers makes fare evasion somewhat challenging. In other words, force.

However, this only works for a limited range of laws, mainly those concerning physical property or people's movement.

Incentives

The broader (and better) solution is not to make law-breaking impossible but to ensure the costs outweigh any temptation that might exist. Here, we are not relying on the power of coercion but instead the power of incentives.

Effective enforcement requires maintaining an environment where the costs of breaking the law outweigh the benefits (or temptations) of doing so.

Benefits / Temptations

Let's face it. In the real world, many short-term benefits or temptations make breaking the law attractive. If I speed a little faster, I won't be late. If I don't perform half of the contract, I keep the benefits without paying. Punching this idiot would feel *really* good.

The temptations are everywhere. The job of an effective law enforcement system is to ensure that, *despite* these temptations, the costs (or sanctions) of lawbreaking are a sufficient deterrent to doing the wrong thing.

Costs / Sanctions

Sanctions are the other side of the coin. They are the consequences of doing the wrong thing – the quiet voice of conscience whispering: "*don't do it*".

The volume with which this voice speaks depends on the severity and likelihood of the sanction occurring.

The *severity* of the sanction is what a hypothetical court would order *if* it found a breach of the law proven. Ten years in prison. Compensation for a broken promise. Giving back what you took.

The *likelihood* of the sanction is how likely a court is to award the sanction. If you speed past a traffic camera, the likelihood is high. Stealing fruit from a country orchid? Pretty low.

While we often associate severity with being the sole measure of a sanction, the reality is that we must consider both severity and likelihood to properly assess the deterrent effect of the law. Even severe punishments will not deter behaviour if they are seldom applied.

For instance, an 'on paper' sanction of $1,000 for fare evasion seems high. However, if there is only a 0.1% chance it will be levied against an offender (because of, for example, a lack of inspectors), it will do little to deter crime. Given the short-term benefits on offer, many people would disregard such a minuscule expected cost ($1, or $1,000 x 0.1%) as practically irrelevant. They would take their chances.

Conversely, even a small token punishment (like a $20 'cleaning charge' for not carrying a towel at the gym) will generally encourage good gym etiquette if enforced every time. The likelihood of a sanction is the driving factor behind high compliance.

Therefore, the likelihood of the sanction must be analysed in conjunction with the severity to get a true sense of the sanction's deterrent effect. We miss the important second half of the equation by focusing on hypothetical headline severity.

Increasing Costs

By policies designed to increase these two constituent elements of sanction (severity and likelihood), we might reasonably expect adherence to the law to increase.

Severity of the sanction

The easiest, cheapest and most expedient way to increase the cost side of the equation and hence encourage compliance with the law is to increase the sanction. Tough new penalties for this. A crack-down approach to that. We can all think of examples.

However, while increasing sanctions is expedient, it can only be pushed so far. All societies maintain an overriding consideration of justice that consequences are proportional to the wrongdoing. A country that relies on draconian punishments to cower citizens into compliance is not generally considered an example of a free and exemplary society.

The death penalty for stealing bread is one way to dissuade theft, but it doesn't speak of an enlightened, developed nation.

Moreover, in a civil context, sanctions (the payment from the defendant to the plaintiff) often cannot be increased past what would be sufficient to fully compensate the injured party. The law generally frowns on civil plaintiffs making an unearned windfall from their litigation.

Likelihood of enforcement

The other, more palatable, way to increase the cost of rule-breaking and hence encourage compliance is to increase the likelihood that the courts will order a sanction. That the offender will be caught and the appropriate consequences levied.

It's just like in sports. If there is a particular behaviour on the field you want to stamp out, you must catch it and punish it with regularity. Players soon get the message when infringements are very likely to be punished.

Increasing the likelihood of punishment means society does not have to make the punishment as extreme. Indeed, the harsh punishments (by today's standards) for theft in the Middle Ages were attributable to the fact that law enforcement was in its infancy, so offenders were not reliably caught. Those unlucky few had to serve as a stern example to the others.

Increasing the likelihood of catching an offender so as not to rely on extreme punishments to encourage law and order is the mark of a mature society. Unlike the severity, it has no upper cap. A 100% success rate is ideal but realistically unachievable. But countries should do their best.

Example

A worked example helps to illustrate how enforcement authorities can manipulate these two levers to achieve better compliance with the law.

Sometimes, merely increasing the penalty is enough, particularly if the penalty was too low originally.

We can take another example from real life – this time from the sport. In the late 1890s, two incidents on the soccer pitch provoked a rule change.

On 20 December 1890, in the Scottish Cup quarter-final between East Stirlingshire and Heart of Midlothian, Jimmy Adams fisted the ball out from under the bar. On 14 February 1891, there was a blatant goal-line handball by a Notts County player in the FA Cup quarter-final against Stoke City.

We can see the instinctive synthesis in these players' minds: commit a foul to save a goal. Given the preciousness of even one goal in soccer (many games finish 0-0), incurring the foul to prevent an otherwise certain goal felt like a fair trade.

The introduction of the penalty rule, whereby an offence in the penalty area (like deliberately handing the ball) led to the attacking team being awarded an unencumbered free shot on goal (with only the keeper to beat), instantly changed the cost-benefit equation. Coupled with a greater propensity of referees to send off the infringing players in these circumstances, the metrics changed. Put simply, the cost of infringing in the penalty area became too high.

As a former (very amateur) player, I can personally attest to the powerful disincentive to foul in this rule's penalty area. Once the ball crosses that magic line, your entire mindset changes from normal play to heightened care and awareness not to commit a foul. I suppose we must attribute the governing body's decision in the late 1890s a success for the long tail of that incentive to pervade into my consciousness even over 100 years later and on the other side of the globe.

In this instance, increasing the penalty alone fixed player behaviour and eradicated a blight on the game.

However, this is a rare example. In most instances, increasing the penalty for breaching the rules is, in and of itself, not a viable way to improve compliance. We need to increase both *penalty* and *severity.*

Take another worked example. Imagine you are the government, and your city has a problem with fare evasion. Too many people aren't paying for a ticket, so trains have insufficient money to run and be maintained regularly. This (unsurprisingly) causes collective grumbling from the citizens.

You try and diagnose the problem. You identify the benefit of not buying a ticket as $10 (the ticket cost – the passenger keeps that money).

Regarding sanctions, the current penalty for fare evasion is $100, and from the statistical analysis, you learn that only 1 in 100 offenders are caught.

From this, the problem is apparent.

Cost = Severity x likelihood = $100 x 1% = $1.

Benefit = $10

The benefits of breaking the law ($10) are ten times the expected costs ($1). No wonder fare evasion is rampant.

What are your options? Clearly, we need to increase the cost of breaking the law to incentivise compliance with it.

There are two options:

1. Increase the penalty; and
2. Increase the likelihood that fare evaders will be caught.

We *could* increase the penalty for fare evasion to $5000, changing nothing else. This means the expected cost of fare evasion would be $5000 x 1% = $50, which is more than the benefit ($10).

This is very expedient and requires almost no effort. However, this is a stern penalty. It would likely lead to allegations of disproportionate justice and unfair scapegoating (it's hard to justify penalising one 'unlucky' person $5,000 while ninety-nine others walk away). An increase in the penalty of this magnitude is probably not viable.

The better option may be a mild increase in the penalty, *combined with* efforts to increase the likelihood of catching evaders. Say we increase the penalty to $250 (a modest and defendable increase) and, through better enforcement efforts, increase the chance of catching an offender to 10%.

Then, the analysis suggests (with time, as the new equation sinks in) that most people *will* purchase a ticket:

Cost = Severity x likelihood = $250 x 10% = $25.

Benefit = $10

In this scenario, the cost of fare evading ($25) outweighs the benefit of doing so ($10). If this state of affairs can be maintained, we expect compliance with the law to improve.

Increasing likelihood

The above analysis shows how important increasing the '*likelihood*' factor in the equation is. How do we increase it?

The likelihood of the court ordering a sanction is highest when someone with sufficient resources, strong evidence, and a clear legal case enforces the law against the defendant.

Therefore, to increase the likelihood of the court issuing a sanction against someone who has broken the law, governments must focus on the following three things:

- Evidence
- Resources
- Clear rules

Clear evidence

Evidence is a necessary precondition of a sanction. All free societies maintain the requirement that an allegation is proved before a court will punish a wrongdoer.

A court must be convinced of the following:

- What happened (so it knows what legal consequence or sanction follows), and
- Who did it (so the law knows whom to levy the sanction against)

Hence, the more evidence available about (1) what happened and (2) who did it, the more likely a sanction will be issued.

For this reason, many countries have policies to ensure such evidence is captured.

Who

In relation to the "who", society collects this information by demanding (among other things) that cars have number plates, gun owners are licenced, and doctors register with a central authority. If something goes wrong, this makes providing the court evidence with convincing evidence of *who* did it (as in, who broke the road rules, who owned the gun, who treated the patient) relatively easy.

On the other hand, sanctions become less likely, and enforcement of the law is frustrated when it is difficult to identify who is responsible for misbehaviour. This can be entirely trivial, like how people treat public bathrooms, to a general annoyance, like unregistered bike riders flouting the road rules, or deliberately nefarious, with bandits wearing masks to avoid identification the classic example.

What

In relation to "what happened", again, society collects this information in the name of maintaining law and order. CCTVs monitor public spaces, and professional observers (patrolling police and security guards) do the same. At the same time, clear business records and organised correspondence serve the same purpose in the private business sphere. It is designed to make (if necessary) evidence of "what happened" readily available to the court. This wall was vandalised with graffiti, a scream was heard from that garage, this person made such-and-such a promise then didn't deliver.

On the other hand, when what happened is not easily observable (such as what caused a disease, what caused a wall to crack, or why a yacht broke its moorings), it is harder to convince a court to order a sanction. How can it, when it's not even sure exactly what led to the disappointing state of affairs? Was it shoddy construction or natural settling? Was it smoking or industrial asbestos exposure? Bad knots or bad luck?

Resolving "what happened" is a critical first step before the court feels comfortable making an order against anyone. Conversely, if the question is shrouded in doubt, it leaves the court paralysed.

You need both

Evidence of "what happened" and "who did it" are key ingredients in the dish of justice. Without one, the whole meal collapses.

The experience of the UK, which now has the highest number of CCTV per capita in the world, is illustrative. Originally installed to assist police in catching violent criminals operating in public spaces (robbers, murderers and other assailants), the experience has been that CCTVs are much more effective at catching and enforcing the more mundane rules of society – traffic laws.

Why is this? We can intuit. In relation to a mugging, CCTV footage may be able to confirm that a mugging did occur. However, unless the footage is exceptionally clear and the orientation of the offender fortuitous, the CCTV does not much assist with identifying "who did it". Without this crucial piece of evidence, a court cannot sanction the wrongdoer. CCTV, therefore, does little to disincentivise muggings for the organised and determined (as opposed to the opportunistic) assailant.

On the other hand, regarding traffic offences, CCTV often provides sufficient evidence for an open and shut case. Consider the evidence it provides: on this date, at this time, a car with these registration plates (who) stopped for 4 minutes and 48 seconds in a no-standing zone (what). In those circumstances, the likelihood of a sanction becomes very likely because the two critical pieces (who and what) of evidence have been captured beyond all arguments.

Hence the experience has been that the presence of CCTV has improved compliance with traffic laws but has not made much of a dint in violent crime. The absence of clear evidence of "who did it" frustrates that latter aim.

Unfortunately, there are no easy answers. Gathering evidence about "who did it" can be difficult. Maybe not for the individual gathering evidence of their business affairs – business dealings are usually with known associates. But for governments seeking to regulate the behaviour of millions (even billions) of individuals, the challenge of monitoring the "*who*" aspect of the equation is particularly acute.

Inevitably, seeking to do so will increasingly intrude on the anonymity of individuals. The obvious objection is how to reconcile a state of increased surveillance with the need for privacy. But perhaps equally, the obvious response screams out: for those who demand privacy, what are you afraid of exposing?

A genuine desire to maintain a sphere of personal and dignified field of privacy should be protected, but "privacy" as a catch-all concept should be rejected when it is simply used as a cloak to hide nefarious behaviour. Transparency promotes good behaviour. Conversely, bad behaviour thrives in the unmonitored nooks, the hidden corners, the sunless recesses and the forgotten places.

In The Adventure of the Copper Beeches, Sherlock Holmes put the matter extremely well. In explaining why he considers the countryside conceals a hidden evil, over the indignation of Watson (who holds a more romantic view of the country), Holmes explains:

> *"The pressure of public opinion can do in the town what the law cannot accomplish. There is no [town] lane so vile that the scream of a tortured child, or the thud of a drunkard's blow does not beget sympathy and indignation among the neighbours, and then the whole vile machinery of justice is ever so close that a word of complaint can set it going, and there is but a step between the crime and the dock.*
>
> *But look at these lonely [country] houses, filled for the most part with poor ignorant folk who know little of the law. Think of the deeds of hellish cruelty, the hidden wickedness which may go on, year in, year out, in such places, and none the wiser."*

Surmising Holmes's characteristically impeccable reasoning with less flourish but greater brevity: scrutiny and crime are inversely related. When scrutiny rises, crime decreases. On the other hand, without scrutiny crime can multiply with abandon (like in the country), as none will be the wiser.

If scrutiny reduces crime, it is inescapable that an increase in privacy will lead to an increase in crime. As mentioned above, a legitimate and defined small sphere of personal privacy is defendable (and indeed entirely appropriate). However, increasing privacy beyond those limits reduces available evidence and makes enforcement of the law harder.

To put it very bluntly, more privacy means more crime. Governments must be clear-eyed about this cost.

People worry that increased surveillance is akin to Big Brother and the beachhead of the development of a police state. But if the laws are just and democratically adopted, and surveillance improves compliance with those laws, it is difficult to see the objection. Those decrying surveillance are usually decrying how it facilitates the enforcement of *unjust* laws promulgated by tyrannical rulers, like in Orwell's 1984. But in a functioning democracy with sensible laws, surveillance (which simply promotes compliance with the law) should not be objectionable. Surveillance, like the police, is just an agnostic enforcement tool. It enforces good and bad laws equally. If you don't like surveillance, you might be complaining about the wrong end of the leash. Perhaps it is the law, not the actual surveillance, which you object to.

It, therefore, behoves the government to invest in monitoring and recording. In a public space, or when conducting public business, there seems to be little available objection to matters remaining inviolably private. After all, drivers on the road might claim a right to "privacy" in order to justify obscuring their number plate (why should the government know where I drive my car?). But we as a society would reject this, as we see that without a visible licence plate, drivers would find it easier to evade the law, making roads significantly less safe for other users.

So, all in all, appropriately calibrated, the benefits of surveillance are clear. The increasing availability of evidence about what happened and who did it increases the likelihood that courts will catch and punish wrongdoers, increasing the deterrent effect of sanctions and improving compliance with the law. And this helps everyone.

Resources for the plaintiff, defendant and the court

Court

Of course, you don't just need evidence. You need somewhere to present it.

Courts must process the cases that come before them accurately and efficiently. Both are critical. Accuracy is essential because society will not accept punishing the innocent. The only reason punishment is tolerated at all, and society accepts jails filled with people, is that we have collective confidence that only people who deserve to be there are there. That there have been no innocent victims inadvertently swept into the system. Accuracy is crucial.

But equally, efficiency is not irrelevant. There is little point in reaching the right result if it takes so long that the criminals' sentence has expired, parties have died, and the world has changed since the event that gave rise to the legal dispute.

In a very practical sense, the reality is that the incentive effect of the law, its primary purpose, loses its potency when the lag between action and outcome, crime and consequence, is so great. A breached contract that takes a decade to get compensation for tends to lose some of its deterrent power.

Of course, the difficulty is a tension between the dual aims of accuracy and efficiency. We need accuracy. But if we favour accuracy above all, an outcome will take unacceptably long.

What's the solution? To answer this, we can have recourse to the universal law of scarcity. They say in picking an outcome, you can have it fast, cheap, or quality – pick two. Undoubtedly, we want a quality decision in a sensible timeframe from the courts. The unavoidable outcome of the law of scarcity says that it will cost us.

If we want quick and accurate, it's therefore going to cost money. Governments must supply it. We cannot demand speed and correctness if society is unwilling to pay for it.

Plaintiff

Someone still needs to get the ball rolling if we've got the evidence and the forum. The plaintiff must have sufficient resources to enforce the law in court.

In historical times, private citizens were expected to enforce the law. If someone broke a contract with you, you had to sue them for damages. If someone murdered you, you (or, more likely, your representatives) had to prosecute the criminal.

Clearly, in some instances, private enforcement remains an important component of enforcing the law. Private citizens are expected to lead the charge (and bear the expense) of enforcing contracts that govern their daily lives. In other instances, however, thinking has evolved, and modern society recognises it would be inappropriate to leave the burden (and the consequential risk that no one would do it) on private citizens. Society has hence developed publicly funded prosecution bodies. Thankfully, no one has to prosecute their murders in these more enlightened times.

Parliaments also sometimes prescribe the creation of specialist bodies to prosecute certain breaches of the law, where it is recognised that the law may not be suitable for private enforcement. The EPA prosecutes environmental destruction. Consumer affairs bodies prosecute for misleading advertising. Corporate watchdogs pursue dodgy company directors. While there often is no in-principle reason why individuals could not sue individually, sometimes it is appropriate that individuals either don't bear the expense or society doesn't take the risk, and the individual will do nothing.

The effectiveness of these bodies cuts both ways. Undoubtedly, they generally have more resources than an individual plaintiff. But equally, no one will care as much and pursue their rights with as much tenacity as the individual who has been wronged.

Defendant

But we mustn't forget. All defendants need to be sufficiently well-resourced (even the ones who did it) to ensure false positives are not caught up in the system.

Clarity about the law

In addition to the court being clear about what happened, there must also be clarity as to whether those facts will be sufficient to bring about a legal finding about a breach of the law. Some laws are straightforward, and there is no doubt. The speed limit is X. You were travelling at X + Y. Fine (in both senses).

But in relation to other laws, there are significant grey areas. The most infamous of these grey areas is laws that require citizens to behave 'reasonably'. The uncertainty as to whether a particular behaviour reaches this standard is apt to introduce uncertainty into the prediction of a court case. This uncertainty undermines the extent to which we can say the outcome of any given legal case will be certain.

This ambiguity is the antithesis of certainty. Ambiguities in the law, therefore, translate to a lower prospect of sanction (even if the facts are incontrovertible) and hence lower adherence to the law. To ensure compliance with the law is encouraged, people need to know the delineating lines of behaviour. It is, therefore, incumbent on legislators of all descriptions to ensure the law is coherent and clear.

The simpler the law, the easier it is to enforce. This reduces costs and helps ensure that everyone who needs to go to court *can* go to court.

Part of achieving simplicity is avoiding the need to tinker unnecessarily. Humans that are passionate about a topic are perennial tinkers. Mechanics and cars. Gardens and roses. Lawyers and the law. But changed words, syntax and commas represent a new opportunity for uncertainty and argument about the application. We must avoid the temptation. Rarely does the law benefit from oblique amendments to a few words. Instead, attention is usually better directed to leaving the law unamended and ensuring it is followed.

Conclusion

Compliance with the law (when using incentives, not force) depends on the costs of lawbreaking outweighing the temptations. While increasing the severity of punishment is part of the picture, the far more palatable (but difficult) limb of the equation is increasing the *likelihood* of the sanction being levied.

To increase the *likelihood*, ensuring that evidence is captured, courts and litigants are well-resourced and clear rules exist are the practical levers at the bottom of the pyramid over which governments have the most control.

Of course, each of these limbs is constantly under threat. Pushes against the leviathan surveillance state. Cutbacks to court budgets. And an ever-multiplying of legislation and court decisions complicating rather than simplifying the rules.

If everyone followed the rules as promulgated, we would have an almost utopian society. There would be no violence, theft and broken contracts – in other words, we would have all the necessary ingredients for a safe, happy and wealthy country. Therefore, instead of directing their attention to social engineering by passing increasingly well-intended prescriptive laws, the government should focus on improving compliance with them.

Of course, incentives will have little role to play in regulating actions committed without thinking (crimes of passion, actions of the mentally encumbered). But this is a small subset. Most humans are, first and foremost, rational and hedonistic – pleasure-seeking and pain-avoiding. If, by the right balance between severity and likelihood, the law can incentivise compliance, compliance with the law should generally be strong, helping us all.

CHAPTER 19 - LEADERSHIP IN LAW

Winston Churchill once said, '*Courage is rightly considered the foremost of the virtues because on it all others depend*'.

Leadership in law is not a function of intelligence, prominence or business-getting ability. The real legal leader embodies productive courage.

Courage is important in three aspects of the law around which our universe revolves:

- Clients
- Courts
- Colleagues

Clients

Courage is required to deal appropriately with clients. Because clients control the revenue and our livelihood, all lawyers must guard against allowing economic considerations to taint our professionalism at all stages of the client life-cycle.

- Getting hired
- Doing the work
- Closing out

Courage is the necessary bulwark against being caught up in economic pressures at each stage.

Getting hired

The endless temptation of the salesperson is to exaggerate (subtly) to get the recalcitrant purchaser across the line.

In law, this manifests as excessive optimism about the client's prospects of winning their case. ('It's a slam dunk!') By inflating the client's expectations, the lawyer generates demand for litigation (if it's a winner, why not?) and positions themselves as the obvious supplier to perform it. Everyone would prefer an optimistic surgeon over a pessimistic one.

But too often, this is a gushing enthusiasm or a sales tactic, not legal advice. The optimism is overstated. It cannot be supported. And being ultimately unsustainable, it ultimately denigrates into nihilistic pessimism as the trial draws near. As the moment of truth approaches and the prospect of making good your inflated earlier promises dawns, suddenly, the tune changes. We've looked at it more. There are risks. You should settle.

This pattern is common and tiresome. We must have the courage to resist it. Calling it as you see it upfront can require giving your potential clients some harsh truth. It may antagonise and will certainly deliver less business. But it is preferable to barracking needless litigation. Courage is key.

Doing the work

As the payer of the bills, clients (especially sophisticated ones) like to be in control. The piper and the tune and all that. A lawyer who is unwilling to do as instructed risks being fired.

But we must have the courage to take this risk, lest we become a mere puppet of the client's whim. A mouthpiece. A gun for hire. Instead, we must keep our eye on the bigger picture: the need for justice, fairness and the rule of law.

The client's interest is in winning. That is our short-term objective, too. But we have a wider consideration and longer-term duty to ensure the system's integrity. To ensure litigation is played fairly and within the rules. So that we can trust that the outcome is just, not merely favourable to us, such as the oath we made on becoming lawyers.

To the extent clients, in their insatiable desire to win, instruct us to depart from this paradigm, we must have the courage to say no. And, if necessary, to part ways. We must bravely stand as independent guardians of the system, not just of the client's narrow and parochial view.

To the extent clients, in their insatiable desire to win, instruct us to depart from this paradigm, we must have the courage to say no.

Finishing up

If you win the case, congratulations. But real courage is required if you lose. The almost overwhelming human reaction is to divert blame for a loss. In sport, it was umpiring. In law, it's that biased jury, those stupid judges or your unethical opponents. But this manifests poor loser syndrome and is both petty and transparent. It is not becoming a dignified profession.

But this is not something the professional appears to have totally outgrown. Take appeals. How many of those are instituted by a damaged ego rather than legal merit? Clearly, not all. But probably too many. Human nature can rarely resist a second opportunity to be proven right.

We must have the courage to avoid this knee-jerk reaction. This is not to argue for easy capitulation. But we must be courageous to accept responsibility rather than deflect blame and consider whether to appeal dispassionately.

Courts

Courageous lawyers appear in court despite unpopular clients and causes.

In the information age, the court of public opinion delivers its verdict much faster than the courts. Acting for those condemned by the public can raise the public ire. But someone has to do it because the court of public opinion is unreliable.

One case that still rankles in the State of Victoria is the 1922 execution of Collin Campbell Ross. Ross was convicted of the rape and murder of a 12-year-old schoolgirl. The public outrage was at a fever pitch. Demands for an urgent conviction. Ross was convicted based on two alleged confessions, and hair samples on his bed said, by nascent forensic science, to match those of the murdered girl.

Ross was convicted, appealed twice unsuccessfully, and swiftly executed. He went to his death bravely, calmly maintaining his innocence.

Ross *was* innocent. DNA tests conducted 80 years later showed that the hairs did not match those of the murdered girl. He was posthumously pardoned. Of course, this was too little, too late. A demand for answers, rushed investigations, fabricated confessions (as they must have been), and unreliable science infinitely compounded the original tragedy.

What Ross, what *society* needed, was a fierce advocate. One is willing to face down public approbation to get to the truth of the matter. To test. To make people pause. To not rush to condemn.

Defending the perceived villains is the only way we can be confident the innocent are not caught up in the fever pitch for retribution. This is the calling of our noble profession. Do we have the courage to take the challenge?

The alternative is to abandon people to the vagrant pit of public opinion, with its terrible whims, thereby irrevocably diminishing our collective humanity.

...defending the perceived villains is the only way we can be confident the innocent are not caught up in the fever pitch for retribution.

Colleagues

Progress is the cost of relevance. We don't expect our houses to be designed on parchment. We don't expect doctors to use leeches, the accountant an abacus, or our bridges to be constructed of mud brick clay. If we want society to continue to embrace and seek our legal expertise, we must move with the times and bring our colleagues along.

Having the idea

The first challenge is to have innovative *ideas*. Innovation sounds high-tech, but it doesn't have to be. The shipping container was innovative, exploding global trade, and that's a metal box. Innovative thinking is a willingness to ask how things could be done differently.

The difficult part is not mastering the latest tech. The hard bit is learning to embrace a new and open mindset. In this respect, lawyers are disadvantaged because of our training and reliance on precedent. Typically, when we are looking at whether we should do something, we look to see whether it has been done before. Novelty, in this sense, is the absolute anathema of good, lawyerly practice.

But novelty, and the intrinsic percentage of failure encumbered with it, is the necessary cost of progress. And continued relevance.

Innovation, therefore, requires us to develop a courageous new way of thinking where we, accepting there will be missteps, step into the unknown as agents of evolution and change.

Selling the idea

That's the first step. Having the idea. The second challenge is getting our colleagues and other lawyers excited about it. This is the *really* hard part. In addition to being a chief innovator and having the idea, we must also be the chief cheerleader and incessantly promote the idea.

We must also be the chief cheerleader and incessantly promote the idea.

Unfortunately, without significant courage, too often, this is an insurmountable barrier. If it's been observed once, it's been observed a hundred times – lawyers are very conservative. Over the totality of the profession, many will inevitably prefer not to change.

The challenge is often manifested as such. The innovator makes a case for change. As is reasonable, they must include reasons and arguments why the proposal is a good one.

But this is like red to a bull for a lawyer. Taking the opposite view is an almost irresistible tendency for any legal mind. Plus, those arguing for *no change* have the clinching argument. Newness is risky, and sameness is safe!

Moreover, there is often an imbued inertia, a facet of every human being (not exclusively lawyers) to overcome. Many people resist change, even in the face of overwhelming logic. *"I hate my job" "Why don't you quit and do something else?" "Oh no, I couldn't do that".*

Hence the predictable cycle of the idea, counter-attack, and reversion to the comfortable status quo. Change comes slowly, if at all.

But without accepting some risk, ancient man would have never ventured past the Pillars of Hercules, the Wright Brothers would not have taken flight, and an unidentified mould growth would not have been developed into penicillin. Risk is the *inescapable cost* of progress. Without some risk, we remain as stranded as those ancients unwilling to sail out past the horizon for fear of the end of the world. We stagnate in our world with our safe boundaries but are frozen in time.

Risk is the inescapable cost of progress. Without some risk, we remain as stranded as those ancients unwilling to sail out past the horizon for fear of the end of the world.

We must therefore have the courage to rise above colleagues' objections, which suck our innovative suggestions back into the quagmire of conservative thinking, to combine the innovator's brilliance with the explorer's courage. To have the stamina, in the face of protest, to push our ideas out of the gravitational pull of traditional thinking that keeps our normal thinking firmly in orbit.

We must never stop advocating for our ideas, push through collective professional inertia, and be ceaseless and tireless advocates for change.

Of course, it's not easy. Taking a concrete, new, public view of something is an occupational hazard for a lawyer. When sticking your head above the collective crowd and saying something novel, you must be prepared for other lawyers to say your idea is unworkable, problematic or even dangerous.

You may even make enemies. But that's the lot of an innovative and visionary leader. As Oliver Emberton said, *"The only way to avoid [annoying] people ... is to do nothing important."*

New ideas in law are always subject to objection from enemies or otherwise.

However, always remember two things. First, the objections are a point of view: nothing more. Do not elevate them to the level of universal truth. And do not get dissuaded solely by another lawyer's reflexive need to take the opposite view. Lawyers are like tennis players – they enjoy themselves much more when they have an opponent to rally against. And lawyers are obstinate. Once committed to a position, they cannot be dislodged except by a judicial decision against them, and even then, they'll often try and argue the toss with appeals and alike. Don't be dissuaded by disagreement – in law, it's inevitable.

Second, progress is the story of persistence. Stick with it, and history may vindicate you. The creator of Spider-Man, Stan Lee, was initially told it was a terrible idea. He ignored that feedback. Ultimately, in 2017, he was able to deliver this sage advice to a graduating class at UCLA:

"If you've got an idea that you genuinely think is good, don't let some idiot talk you out of it."

The right balance

Being a champion of change clearly requires courage and foresight, but we must also imbue the role with another trait: fairness. Too many would-be revolutionaries trip here. When arguing for change, we must avoid falling into the trap of vehemently rubbishing everything in the existing system.

Some (not all, but some) elements of our legal system are the way they are and have been so for a long time because they *are* effective. To take but a simple example: the concept of the separation of powers between the legislature, executive and judiciary has been around in a formalised sense at least since the American Declaration of Independence, and as an overarching structural element of the legal profession, it works well. There are others – trial by jury, right to silence, professional independence and alike – which have served, do serve and will serve us well into the future.

In advocating for change, we should be slow to conclude that everything is broken and even slower to argue for total revolution and the elimination of the current system.

The balance, I think, is this. The profession is based on two foundations: the timeless and the contemporary. The timeless aspects (independence, loyalty, competence) do not require updating because they are, by definition, timeless. Leave these alone. The contemporary aspects (modes of communication, techniques at trial, barriers to practising, etc.) can and should constantly be evolving. Here, our advocacy efforts are most appropriate and most likely to be effectual. But remember, to be most effective, such advocacy needs to be an exercise in quiet and persistent persuasion rather than revolutionary rabble-raising.

In our necessary evolutionary push, we must show proper deference and respect for what has come before. It can appear as youthful arrogance to simply argue for the jettisoning of long-standing concepts. We must treat change with respect. Like altering an old family recipe – yes, it might have to be updated (why bake over coals when we have ovens?), but argue your case slowly and gently. Or like taking advice from our grandparents. Respect their wisdom, politely defer, and only then pass their advice through the prism of contemporary society to decide what is well-intended but outdated.

In addition to *what* to change, there is also the question of technique, of *how* we try to change it. Caution is necessary here, too.

When seeking to dislodge the status quo, it is very tempting to descend into vehemence, exaggeration and hyperbole. It's the instinct of a litigator to completely rubbish those on the other side of the argument (their entire case is "barking mad!"). But this tends to make people justifiably defensive, using an understandable rejection of your criticism framed in totalitarian terms to avoid the undeniable kernels of truth.

If you want your spouse to assist with more with the housework, it is generally unhelpful to say, "you're lazy and never help". This ineffectively, in our annoyance, expands the truth and entrenches our foe. "You don't help enough" is a little better. "I have been tracking our chores over the last week, and here are my findings. How do you think we can better balance the load?" is best. A fair, evidence-based argument for change.

Slogan-based soapbox advocacy may be catchy and easy but is not ineffective compared with the careful, evidence-based promotion of change. Our legal intuition serves us well in this respect.

Conclusion

Courage is key. The courageous lawyer showing leadership and integrity with clients, courts and colleagues can leverage that courage into significant good.

And courage is not as hard as you think. The difference between the brave person and the coward is that the brave person hangs in there for five seconds more. Nor does the responsibility have to rest on any one set of shoulders. We can all make an effort to add small acts of courage to our everyday practice. No one will likely notice. A few thanks will be received. Being courageous may be a lonely challenge.

But true courage is a virtue for its own sake and doesn't require the promise of praise or recognition to extract it.

We should do it, regardless of whether observed. Because the compounding effect of small, anonymous acts of everyday courage spread widely across the profession would have as much impact as any one legal Caesar, Lincoln or Napoleon at the helm.

CONCLUSION

This book has run the gambit from the immensely practical (what am I doing: advising or advocating) to the remote and speculative (how we, as legal leaders, have an obligation to concoct and champion innovative ideas that may utterly change the complexion of the profession). Yet despite the seeming diffuse lens of focus, I have consciously attempted to present the ideas linearly from least to most expansive.

There is a reason for this. Maslov popularized the hierarchy of needs, whereby we must first ensure our most pressing and basic survival needs are met before we can turn our attention to larger and more esoteric goals like changing the world. And I think the model commends itself to our work as well.

First, we must take care of our work now. We must identify, with clarity, whether we are advocating or advising, what happened, and what type of dispute we have. From this foundation, we can then turn our attention to *creativity* – coming up with the winning argument. This maximises the client's value by increasing the chance of prevailing in court or settling on advantageous terms. And in following this process, we must not neglect the immense power of working as a team.

Second, we can get more expansive once our basic pressing needs are met. How do we win the next interesting case where we can help someone? As discussed, this requires we (1) intellectually accept the need to market and then (2) get over our fear of rejection (or be helped over it by others). In addition, in attempting to prove we are the best lawyer for the job, we should consider providing proof in the form of available statistics.

Once our engagement is secured, we must consider how we will charge. Most of the time, the billable hour is appropriate and not the evil it is sometimes accused of. In narrower situations, a fixed fee or even no-win, no-fee arrangements (among others) might be considered. Regardless of the fee selected, if the law wants to remain affordable and accessible, we as a profession might need to consider alternative ways of doing things (including hard caps).

Third, and finally, once we have won this case and established the right to the next, we can relax our minds from the pressing needs of today and start considering some of the bigger issues of the future. As a justice system, do we appropriately respond to our users' time, cost and quality needs? How can we make our law firms stronger, happier and more effective organisations by nurturing internal relationships? How can enforcing the law assist our entire society, and how can we carefully pull the levers on incentives to encourage greater adherence to the same? And what of the need to be courageous, the 'foremost of the virtues', where we, as lawyers, behave with courage with current clients and the courts, as well as showing bravery in leading (and dragging) others into the future?

In doing so, in progressing from the pressing to the more philosophical, we give ourselves the best hope of being professionals of impact. Maslov would observe that it's difficult to change the world if we don't have enough to eat. Similarly, it's difficult to change the legal world unless we first have mastered the basics of winning this case and securing the next case (which, in reality, is our next meal).

But having conquered the immediate and pressing needs, we can open up our thoughts and present to the world with our infinite capacity for good ideas. To be agents of massive systemic change rather than simply careful professionals with a narrow range of vision.

Good luck.

ACKNOWLEDGEMENTS

This is my first book, and naturally, with any 'first', I can observe three things.

First, this book, my first foray into the world of publishing, will always hold a particularly special place in my heart. It is the apex of many hours, countless revisions, and occasional loss of heart, but ultimate completion, and will always be a source of pride as I look at it sitting on the shelf, and perhaps, if I am lucky, being read by a few people here and there.

Second, as with any 'first time', there is an initial hurdle to overcome: the fear and trepidation we all feel when diving into the unknown. Quivering at the top of the diving board as a child. Hesitating to make the first move in a new romance. Wondering where you should sit on Day One of school. It's a common human insecurity, and I am grateful for three Davids in assisting me in surmounting that initial hurdle.

First, David Thomson, who first instilled a love of the law, driven by his relentless passion, was my Year 10 Legal Studies teacher. Thank you for giving 16-year-old Sam a taste of "yes, this is *it* – what I want to do with my life". I am forever grateful for the world you opened up to me (and countless other equally grateful students of yours).

Second, David Simpson, my first proper mentor, whose simple observation when I was 29 that 'you could write a book' opened my eyes to an exciting new possibility. I distinctly remember thinking, "of course, why not?" In hindsight (as is always the case), it shouldn't have taken a nudge from someone else, but it did, and I am forever grateful to David for giving it to me.

The final David is David Maister, a writer, consultant and guru on all things professional service firms. I admire his writings. Through his works, he showed me that the best books are rigorous and readable, as well as being peppered with softer, relatable moments and autobiographical asides. I gratefully acknowledge his important influence on the development of my own style.

Finally, as is the case with anything described as being 'first', it presupposes there will be at least a second (otherwise, it properly morphs from being described as first to *only*). The preparation of this book, written alongside my 'day job' of being a litigation lawyer, has been the source of much enjoyment, a dash of frustration, and ultimately a glowing feeling of professional satisfaction. Therefore, I can say this: first, yes, but certainly not last. There may be a second edition and further books, but the writing process has given me immense energy and joy, and I don't intend to stop.

It is my privilege to be able to share this book with you, my reader, and I hope the enjoyment this book has given me permeates through to you in as many places as I have permitted it to leak out.

ABOUT THE AUTHOR

Samuel J. Woff is a commercial construction lawyer, construction litigation specialist, speaker, author and consulting academic at Melbourne University.

He lives in Melbourne's bayside with his wife, Jenny.

Printed in Dunstable, United Kingdom

91220884R00137